The Godprint

Navigating Life His Way

Ebony Robinson

Copyright © 2017 Ebony Robinson

Unless otherwise indicated, all Scripture quotations are taken from the Holy Bible, King James Version (Public Domain).

ISBN: 978-0-9863813-7-9 (Paperback)

ISBN: 978-0-9863813-8-6 (E-book)

BM Webster Publishing, LLC.

For more information about scheduling the author for speaking engagements, or book discounts please contact the author at the email address provided: 320rise@gmail.com

ALL RIGHTS RESERVED. This book contains material protected under International and Federal Copyright Laws and Treaties. Any unauthorized reprint or use of this material is prohibited. No part of this book may be reproduced or transmitted in any form or by any means, electronic or mechanical, including photocopying, recording, or by any information storage and retrieval system without express written permission of the publisher, except in the case of brief quotations embodied in critical reviews and certain noncommercial uses permitted by copyright law. For permissions requests, write to the publisher, addressed "Attention: Permissions Request," at the email address provided: Publishing@itsBrittneyMichelle.com.

Table of Contents

14 Day Devotional

Foreword

I remember the times like it was literally yesterday. I had just graduated from college and was still into hip hop major. The summer of 2001 for those who love hip hop were awaiting the release of the new Jay–Z Album. This was when an album release date still meant something. Unfortunately, the release date: September 11, 2001 was overshadowed by the attack on our country, and demise of the World Trade Center in New York City. This album by Jay–Z would be named "Blueprint". The "Blueprint" was Jay–Z's fourth studio album, and like the title, proved to be the formula for how to make a classic rap album. Just like the 'Blueprint', the 'Godprint' by Ebony Robinson makes a big claim. That claim is that a successful life of Godly living is not happen stance or coincidence, but it follows a blueprint, rightly titled by Ebony Robinson as the 'Godprint'. The premise of the book is that God is not a respecter of persons and everyone who follows the principles of having an abiding relationship with him will succeed at that cause.

The Godprint is not just another book on Christian Living. This book is unique in that Ebony takes time to breakdown time tested principles in language that young and old can relate. She goes to much effort to make sure that the reader feels comfortable and confident to follow the principles being laid out in this book. She does this by making the complex digestible no matter where you are on your spiritual journey. She proves in this book that culture, trends and times change; but the basics of leading a successful life with Christ will always remain the same. Leonardo Da Vinci stated that, 'Simplicity is the ultimate sophistication'. By using her own life, she makes the pages come alive with her practical but profound insights.

As a Pastor, I was greatly helped and encouraged by the 'Godprint'. But, I must admit I may be a little biased. Not only is Ebony a member of Reach Church in Ypsilanti, MI where I Pastor, but she is also my wife of 12 years. But for me therefore, the 'Godprint' makes even more impact on me. I have seen Ebony live every word that is contained within the pages of this book. She has been a faithful wife, loving mother, minister and business owner. The heart that is displayed especially towards women is real and authentic. She has mentored, coached, and helped so many live Godly as women.

The uniqueness of this work in its application is that it can be read as an encouragement, but it is also written to be a tool for teaching and training. Although it may not take much time to read this gem of a book, it will be one where you will want to keep close to reference continuously as a guide to a blessed life. Not to mention this work is entertaining and engaging with real life examples and interesting word play. Ebony did a great job of representing herself as a disciple of

Christ, but also writing this work in a conversational style that is engaging until the last word.

So, who should read this book and why? The first person who should read this book is someone without a clue. Before you say that you are offended by that description, let me be the first to admit that I spent the first 24 years of my life clueless. Because I was unclear on who God made me to be, every decision and opportunity was complicated and confusing because I was unsure about who God created me to be. By following the principles in this book, you will gain a greater sense of clarity and purpose as your relationship with God grows.

Secondly the person who is looking to maximize your days should read this book. We only get one life, and I believe that deep down, we all desire to leave a legacy of good works behind. Ebony shows us that the major step in leaving that legacy behind is first our contentment and peace that comes through having a 'Godprint'. Whether your work is inside or outside of traditional ministry, a sure intimate plan to grow with God will guide you step by step.

The third person who should read this book is someone who takes the 'Great Commission' seriously. In the Bible; Matthew 28:19,20 Jesus tells his disciples, "Therefore go and make disciples of all nations, baptizing them in the name of the Father and of the Son and of the Holy Spirit and teaching them to obey everything I have commanded you. And surely, I am with you always, even to the end of the world." We are commanded to make disciples of Christ. This book is a great disciple making tool for the new or mature believer.

In closing, if you are serious about growing in God and don't want to risk your future on chance, read and re -read the Godprint. It is already a proven plan to a successful purposeful life.

Pastor Jason Robinson

Reach Church

www.reachchurchypsi.org

Preface

This book has been a labor of love. I have always known that I had a book inside of me, but was always nervous to put it on paper. To put my thoughts on paper for the masses to read was quite nerve-wrecking. Who would want to read what I had to say? – I could hear that inner voice tell me constantly. So, I finally allowed the Holy Spirit to win the war that was raging on the inside. I pray this book blesses you immensely and challenges you tremendously. -Ebony

Let's stay connected:

Follow me on social media @ebonylrobinson

For bookings please email 320rise@gmail.com.

Acknowledgments

I want to thank God for being a true and living God. With Him all things are possible, and I am a testimony as to this fact. Even when I am not the best daughter to my Heavenly Father, He still loves me unconditionally. I am so grateful for Jesus Christ who died for me knowing who I would be – undeserving of such a beautiful movement of love in action. I am thankful for the Holy Spirit who resides in me and directs my steps. I acknowledge being a mess, but I am humbled for it becoming a message.

My parents always pushed me to be more, to be better, to think for myself, and to be me in a sea of copies. My mother, Belinda, was such a spicy lady. Even though she is not here on Earth, her legacy lives within me. We spoke about a lot of things before she passed. She knew I was writing this book, and was quite interested. She wanted to know where I was in the process when we talked, and she probably wanted to tell me what to write too. I didn't finish it before her passing, but I know she was with me. Momma, this book is for you. I am grateful for parents who allowed me to figure out my passion, believed that what they instilled in me will reap long-term benefits, and took me to church every Sunday. My Dad, AJ, is a great Earthly Father, and I could not have chosen such a great man as my Dad.

My dear brother, Anthony, is the best brother for me. I have countless stories on how he has impacted my life, but the best is when I was in the eighth grade and he was a senior in high school. I was confident that I could beat him in a foot race. So, on the hard street I put on my track spikes – don't ask – and lined up to race. He gave me a head start, but he still beat me. I was VERY upset, I mean REALLY upset. I honestly thought I could beat him. Even though I was younger and weaker, (he was a defensive lineman) he did not take it easy on me. He taught me that in life - people may be better than you, but always have the confidence to be competitive and to get back up when you lose. You will lose, but character is built in those moments of adversity. Also, I have a gained a great sister in my brother's wife, Kim. Thanks for loving my brother and keeping him together.

My little sister, Constance, is just precious. The biggest gem from her is not to make a conclusion based on a caterpillar. The process is still happening, and a beautiful butterfly will shine. Fly my beautiful butterfly.

I have an excellent group of women in my life who has my back, I can be very transparent with, and loves me despite my flaws. Thank you, Alexis, Cynitra, Kara, Kimberle, Kimberly, Mirada, and Tracy.

To my Eastern Michigan University and University of Michigan babies, I love you!

Acknowledgments

Reach Church, Ypsilanti, MI. What a great congregation. When God spoke to my husband to plant His church, I wasn't sure what that would mean for our family and my life. I am so grateful for what Reach is and who she is becoming. Every person who is a part of Reach, thank you for allowing the Holy Spirit to move you to join us in His magnificent work. Because of your obedience, we are living out the mission – Where the Lost are Found, the Found are Equipped, and the Equipped are Sent. @reachchurcha2y www.reachchurchypsi.org.

Thank you, Dr. Addis Moore, for training and teaching me as a young woman. Grateful for your view that women can and are called to the ministry. My time spent under your tutelage was life changing.

My children – Naima, Tahirah, Solomon, and Sanaa. Being a parent is a challenge and rewarding. I have matured so much as I love you and you love me.

Finally, Jason. My husband loves me more than I deserve – to be very forthright. Meeting you at 18 years old, I knew you were meant to be in my life for our lifetime. So much to say, but these verses sums it up.

> Husbands, love your wives, just as Christ also loved the church and gave Himself for her, that He might sanctify and cleanse her with the washing of water by the word, that He might present her to Himself a glorious church, not having spot or wrinkle or any such thing, but that she should be holy and without blemish. So husbands ought to love their own wives as

their own bodies; he who loves his wife loves himself. Ephesians 5:25-28 (NKJV)

Introduction

As a young woman, I always knew I wanted more. I wanted to be more and I wanted to do more, but I did not know how to do that. I knew I wanted to make some changes in my life, but I didn't have a mentor or a person who I could bounce ideas off of or ask questions. So, I always reverted to my safe zone – church. I was raised in church, but honestly did not understand who God really was. I understood that He made Heaven and Earth. I understood Jesus Christ came to Earth to die for me. I understood that if I confessed Romans 10:9 (NIV) which says, "If you declare with your mouth, 'Jesus is Lord,' and believe in your heart that God raised him from the dead, you will be saved," I would be good. And yet, I still wasn't *good*. I kept telling myself there had to be more. I was a regular in church – I didn't follow every command though. I definitely did things I should not have done (Thank You Father for your grace and mercy). I was a tither. Yes, I gave 10% of my income consistently, even when I didn't go to church. I honestly tried to live "right," but... nothing.

Living, experience, and years later – I FINALLY GOT IT! Living an abundant life wasn't all about the money, shoes, clothes, (those are nice things to have – don't get it twisted) but it was wrapped up in having an intimate, personal relationship with Him. It started there! It finally made sense as to why I took off from the starting line, and wound up in the wrong lane. It made sense why things seemed so superficial. It made sense why I was running so hard, exerting all my energy and going nowhere. The answer: I really didn't know my Creator. How crazy was that? I'm sure He desired to have a relationship with me, but I never fully stopped to meet Him.

"Hello Father my name is Ebony, and I want to get to know you."

"Hello Ebony I have been patiently waiting on you. I'm so glad that you finally stopped to pay attention to Me. I have so much to tell you and show you. Are you ready?"

"Yes, Father. I am ready."

Does that sound like you? Go ahead girl, raise your hand!

The purpose of this book is for you to have a blueprint of how to lead a successful, God-centered life. Stop wasting your time. Stop wandering aimlessly. Stop living a life that you were not meant to live. Are you ready to transform? Are you ready for change? You know there is more, right? Do you want it? Come on girl, let's go get it together. Run, do NOT walk. As you read this book take notes, re-read a chapter, and highlight sections that speak to you. This is your opportunity to come out of the shadows, transform your life, and step into your destiny.

Chapter One

Daddy's Girl

Establishes and Develops a Personal Relationship with God

The joys of dating... or NOT. Going to all the parties, after-sets, and get-togethers just to meet people. Once you meet someone that meets your expectations (at least the minimum from your 50-bullet point list) you both decide to go out on a date. Since you halfway think he's decent in the face, you go all out with the preparation. You call the squad to help you get your game up. At the end of the squad session your hair is laid, eyebrows on fleek, face beat (make up looks nice -- not domestic violence, Lordy!), fashion is on trend, and new bag is poppin' -- selfie game strong. Now you are on the date. So many questions to ask and to answer, so much information to take in, so much to decide. Dating can be so much fun, but it is so much work.

What is dating anyway? Dating is when two people meet socially with the aim of each assessing the other's suitability as a partner in a more committed, intimate relationship or marriage. Lots of time, effort, and money is spent on dating – trying to establish a relationship with that potential mate. Are you someone who wants and yearns to date, yet skimps out on establishing a relationship with the Creator, the One who made you? The One who knows all about you. The One who loves you. The one relationship that will never, ever fail. Deuteronomy 31:8 says, "And the Lord, He is the One who goes before you. He will be with you, He will not leave you nor forsake you; do not fear nor be dismayed." Your Heavenly Father wants a relationship with you. Revelations 3:20 says, "Behold, I stand at the door and knock. If anyone hears My voice and opens the door, I will come in to him and dine with him, and he with Me." Don't you want a relationship with Him? Aren't you tired of relationships that never live up to your expectations? Aren't you over that dude who keeps saying that you are "the one" but never steps up to the plate? Aren't you looking for a relationship with someone who longs to be with you? It's time to establish a relationship with God.

How to Establish a Relationship

People have asked me, "Ebony, how do I get close to God?" Or, they repeat the sentiment that says, "I've fallen off the wagon and I just don't know how to get back on." We want to have this amazing relationship out the gate. It's like as young girls, we envisioned this beautiful wedding: Bridesmaids and Maid/Matron of honor... exquisite, one-of-a-kind gown... gorgeous. We've even gone as far as to plan who's going to sing, but we forget that we need to get a mate to have the wedding. We get so far ahead of ourselves, then we feel defeated because it seems like it's an impossible task. I had a boss who once asked me, "How do you eat an elephant?" I'm thinking, "Is this a trick...ummm... carefully?" The answer was – "one bite at a time." The same goes with your relationship with Christ. How does it get established? The answer: one step at a time. Don't compare yourself to others, just walk your walk. What I love about walking is that as you get closer, God illuminates things, people, ideas, your steps, and you see the plan He has for you. Jeremiah 29:11-12 says, "For I know the plan I have for you, declares the Lord, plans to prosper you and not to harm you, plans to give you hope and a future. Then you will call on me and come and pray to me and I will listen to you." When you get closer you then know who He is, which in turn shows you who you are and who you are not. When you know you are an eagle, you don't kick it with vultures. You don't hang out with those who are going in the opposite direction you are going in, you know?

He, our Heavenly, loving Father, desires to be close to you, but many times we reject His advances. You know, like that guy who's trying to step to you, and you keep throwing him shade. We do that with our Father, it's just not as obvious as what we do to the guy. He created us to praise Him and to follow the path He has ordained for us. He is always drawing closer, but we have to do our part. God has given us free will; however, it is important for us to follow the instruction manual - the Bible. The B-I-B-L-E. We must have the desire to learn more of, and seek a relationship with the Creator. Now don't get all super excited because you start believing Christ is a genie in the bottle and no issues will come your way. Baby! We will have problems. II Timothy 3:12 NIV keeps it real all the way real with us. "In fact, everyone who wants to live a godly life in

Christ Jesus will be persecuted." So don't get this Christian life twisted. Though trouble may come, having a relationship with God allows us to talk, ask questions, pour our hearts out to Him, and listen to Him as He speaks. He gets our attention in many ways, but are we listening and watching? Just like we had a desire for that man or material things, we should have a deeper desire, a longing, for our God. This must be private and personal. So how do you establish the relationship? Well, girl, it's not that complicated. We just make it so complicated. Sometimes we want things to be so deep, and thankfully, in this case it's not that hard or deep. Get out of the deep water, and come on in to the shore. So how do we do it? These are in no order, but when applied consistently and congruently, will put you on the right path.

Meditate

The common perception of meditation is comprised of incense, breathing, concentrating on nothing, being still, etc. Well, that was my perception. I felt like I needed to be in a room sitting on a mat on the floor, with some yoga pants on and my hair in a head wrap. While the bible doesn't give us a dress code for meditation, it does tell us when it should be done. Psalm 1:2 says, "His delight is in the law of the Lord, and in His law he meditate day and night." The verb "meditate" carries this meaning: "murmuring continually and pondering deeply". Meditating on the Word is a focused repetition of phrases from the Scripture.

This is the process I use when I meditate:

- Read it
- Write it
- Say it
- Listen (to the Holy Spirit)
- Repeat

Read the verse several times. You may even want to have access to multiple translations for understanding. Write it down exactly how it is written in the bible. Yes, write it down. I know you may be thinking, who writes anymore? Well, writing things down helps with processing the information. Say the verse aloud with boldness and confidence. Don't be afraid to speak the Word. Listen for connecting thoughts from God through the Word. God will surely speak, so be sure to listen attentively. Repeat this process until you know that you have received the message, the lesson, the direction, or the decision needed.

The next question that is probably bubbling up in your mind is, "What I should meditate on?" Such a great question my dear, I'm so glad you asked. The verse that you choose (or chooses you) should be specific to the situation in your life. So, I cannot give you a verse, (don't close the book on me) but I can tell you to meditate on truth. Philippians 4:8 says, "Finally, brethren, whatever is true, whatever is honorable, whatever is right, whatever is pure, whatever is lovely, whatever is of good repute, if there is any excellence and if anything worthy of praise, dwell on these things." Many times, we're meditating/dwelling/concentrating on the wrong things.

What have you been meditating on? Are you meditating on negativity? Are you meditating on drama? Hear me - that negative crap gets in our spirits and minds, and it becomes this heavy cloud over us. You start to drag a little, the pep in your step goes away, and the smile on your face turns upside down, all because of negative concentration. But, I just love the Word of God because it tells us to meditate on what is true, honorable, right, pure, lovely, and of good repute. What does that mean? It means that you are fearfully and wonderfully made (Psalm 139:14). That you are more than a conqueror (Romans 8:37). That you are complete in Christ (Colossians 2:10). That you are a royal priesthood (I Peter 2:9). That He who began a good work in you will carry it on to completion until the day of Jesus Christ (Philippians 1:6). That you have been appointed for a great work (Jeremiah 1:5). That you were bought with a price (I Corinthians 6:20a). That you are His workmanship (Ephesians 2:10). That you are a friend of God (John 15:15). That you are the light of the world (Matthew 5:14). You meditate on what the Word of God says, not what someone else says, or even what the situation looks like. Boom! Message! Take that stinking thinking - you have to go. The next piece to the puzzle is to study.

Study

"Why should I study the bible?" you may be asking yourself. Who "studies" the bible? Let me hit you with a scripture. II Timothy 2:15 says, "Study to show thyself approved unto God, a workman that needeth not to be ashamed, rightly dividing the word of truth." The Message translation says, "Concentrate on doing your best for God, work you won't be ashamed of, laying out the truth plain and simple." When a person knows the Word, they can discern what is truth and what is not. That is so critical because it gives direction. We are being tested on a consistent basis, but it has been difficult for us to pass because we do not know the answer. The interesting thing is that these tests are open book. I can remember being in school and people would be geeked about open book tests. Yes geeked! Believe it or not people would still fail. Why? Because even though it was an open book test, you still needed to have been familiar with the information to be able to find it in the book. Preach! The answers are in the book – the Word of God. There are school answers, job answers, relationship answers, and life answers all in the book. I heard a Pastor, Reverend Kirbyjohn Caldwell of Houston, Texas say, "We are smart in the world, but very dumb as Christians and in the church." For us to be successful we have to know the material. So why should you study? Because your life literally depends on it. Did she just say that? Yes, I just said that. And guess what? I meant it. Your life AND the life of someone else literally depends on you being well versed in the Word of God. How do you study? Just like you would study subject matter for school or your job. Remember earlier when I said it is not that complicated? I know it may seem daunting. Some of the words are tough to pronounce! But, that should not steer you away from the importance of studying His Word. There are many ways to study the Word of God, but I will show you through various steps that are effective for me and many others.

First, you want to set aside time to study. You may need to schedule an appointment in your preferred planner tool. At the beginning it may not happen every day – maybe it is every other day for 20 minutes. That is just fine. You cannot compare your study time to Bishop T.D. Jakes! Do not compare apples to oranges. Just do you! Believe me, as you get in His Word your time will increase. Eventually you will become so excited that you will lose track of time, but you must start somewhere. Next, you want the space to be favorable to studying. That can mean different things to different people. For me, it's a nice quiet space that is well lit. I cannot have any background noise, because the smallest amount of noise will break my concentration. You may like to study in a coffee shop, library, or an atypical studying setting. Know yourself and do what works for you, the key is to avoid distractions. Turn off every device, turn off push notifications, or turn the phone to silent. Third, just like class you want to have all your study material readily available. The materials you need to study the Word may include: the Bible, a writing instrument, highlighter, notebook, concordance (contains an alphabetical index of words used in the Bible and the main Bible references where the word occurs), and a bible dictionary. These materials will set you up for a successful study session. Lastly, (or maybe this should be first), you want to pray before you open the Bible. You want your heart to be softened before you start studying. Nothing can enter hard ground, and the same goes with your heart and spirit. You want to be clear of drama, and rid yourself of the toxins from the day or the night before, before you start studying. Finally, the third piece to the puzzle is prayer. This is about to get good (or get better)!

Pray

God has commanded us to pray, for it is the way that we communicate with Him. Many times, we think it is a way for us to call Him up and tell Him what we want, and then hang up. No, communication is a 2-way thing! Prayer allows us to worship and praise the Lord. It also allows us to offer confession of our sins, which should lead to our genuine repentance. Moreover, prayer grants us the opportunity to present our requests to God. He is personal, cares for us, and wants to commune with us through prayer. Hebrews 4:15-16 reads, "For we do not have a high priest who is unable to sympathize with our weaknesses, but we have one who has been tempted in every way, just as we are - yet was without sin. Let us then approach the throne of grace with confidence, so that we may receive mercy and find grace to help us in our time of need." Prayer is not just about asking for God's blessings – though we are welcome to do so – but it is about communication with the living God. Without communication, relationships fall apart. You know that feeling when you finally get a chance to hang out with your friend, but you haven't really spoken to each other in a while? There is often a feeling of awkwardness. It becomes so awkward that you become distant, and the relationship starts to fizzle. Have you been there before? It all falls down. Similarly, our relationship with God suffers when we do not communicate with Him. So how do you pray? People may say you should start by saying "XYZ," make sure you mention "ABC,"come back around and thank God for "123," sprinkle in "DEF," and end with "LMNOP." That's helpful, right? Not really. You may be saying I've never prayed before or seriously prayed. There's this scripture in the bible, Romans 8:26-27 AMP that says:

> "So too the [Holy] Spirit comes to our aid and bears us up in our weakness; for we do not know what prayer to offer nor how to offer it worthily as we ought, but the Spirit Himself goes to meet our supplication and pleads on our behalf with unspeakable yearnings and groanings too deep for utterance. And He Who searches the hearts of men knows what is in the mind of the [Holy] Spirit [what His intent is], because the Spirit intercedes and pleads [before God] in behalf of the saints according to and in harmony with God's will."

That is good news, right? When you are unsure of what to say, the Holy Spirit intercedes on your behalf. There are times I just say, "Ok God I need you, please help me. You may be there... Lord Help!" There is no canned approach that you need to take, just talk from your heart. There is the ACTS model that may be helpful to get you to rev up your engines. ACTS stands for Adoration, Confession, Thanksgiving, and Supplication. The first term, Adoration means worship. Praise the Father for who He is and for all that He has done for you. Sample: "God I praise you for being a Mighty God and being everything that I need."

Confession, the second component, means agreeing with God about the things that you have done wrong. Ask God to forgive you for these things, and then believe that He does so freely. Sample: "God I thank you for being a forgiving God. I realize that my actions (INSERT WHAT YOU KNOW TO BE AGAINST GOD'S WILL) were not of you and I repent and fall on my knees asking for your forgiveness, and I forgive myself, freeing myself from any guilt and shame." Third is Thanksgiving, which means being thankful to God. Thank Him for what He has done in your life. Sample: "God I thank you for (SOMETHING SPECIFIC THAT YOU ARE SURE THAT GOD DID). Because of you blessing me I am able to (WHAT CAN YOU NOW DO BECAUSE OF GOD'S GRACIOUS ACTION TOWARD YOU?)".

Supplication is the final component and means, praying for your needs and for the needs of others. Sample: "Father I am standing in the need of (INSERT NEED). Your Word says that you will never leave me nor forsake me. I am standing in the gap for my dear friend. God, you know her every need but I am petitioning you to (EXPRESS SPECIFIC NEED). God, she is leaning and depending on you. In Jesus Name, I pray Amen."

Putting these pieces together makes a great puzzle. The key is to do these things – meditate, study, and pray – consistently. You don't put makeup on half of your face and think it's cute. It's not- it must be done correctly, starting with the right foundation. The same is true with establishing a relationship with the Father – build the right foundation. Our actions however, are quite the contrary because we want the end result – a successful life – without being consistent with the elementary things. Establish your relationship with your Heavenly Father, He is waiting.

How to Develop a Relationship

It may take time to establish a relationship with The Father, but once you do, the work doesn't end there. You must be intentional about developing and strengthening that relationship. Continue to meditate, study, and pray along with what is in this section. Don't tune me out or put the book down. Yes, it sounds like a lot on top of everything else you have going on in your life, but baby girl remember, you said you wanted more. To reach the level of achievement you must put effort into it.

I attend Reach Church in Ypsilanti, Michigan. Well my relationship to Reach Church is more than just an attendee – my husband is the Pastor (smile). At Reach, we have this model that is called the 'Road to Growth'. We believe that scripture shows that true spiritual growth and life maturity comes not by one event, but by obedience and consistency over time. Jesus tells us in John 8:31, "If you continue in my Word, then you are truly disciples of mine; and you will know the truth, and the truth will make you free." Ironically, developing your relationship with Christ involves other people. I Corinthians 12:14, 18NIV says, "Even so the body is not made up of one part but of many. [18] But in fact God has placed the parts in the body, every one of them, just as he wanted them to be." Go figure! For a plant to grow it takes more than just sunlight – it takes the sum of water, sun, soil (and probably other stuff I learned in elementary school) for growth. So, get out of your quiet space at home and follow this process.

First you want to **Gather**. This means to consistently attend worship service. I understand you have a lot going on in your life, and you feel as if you cannot commit to being consistent. As I stated earlier YOUR life and SOMEONE else's life depends on you. You consistently get on social media, go to work, and go to school, so the act of consistency is in you. Please make the sound choice to be consistent in this area as well. Hebrews 10:25 NIV says, "not giving up meeting together, as some are in the habit of doing, but encouraging one another – and all the more as you see the Day approaching." You want to find a local church that is teaching the Bible and applies the Word. Ask your colleagues, classmates, friends, or former Pastor about local churches that fit that description. Let me push this point: FIND A LOCAL CHURCH THAT TEACHES THE BIBLE. It is quite all right to have an opinion or a belief, but it is critical that the opinion or belief matches the Word of God.

Secondly, you want to **Connect**. This means to join and actively participate in a life group and/or a bible study group. Being connected to other believers is so important. You know how you crave being around your girlfriends? That is the craving you should have as a believer. There is love in the fellowship (I John 4:12). You are not meant to live life lonely, so don't voluntarily be a lone ranger. Do life with other like-minded people. So what does do life with someone mean? The closest biblical phrase that matches "doing life together" is found in Psalm 133:1NIV, which says, "How good and pleasant it is when God's people live together in unity." The word 'live' in this verse is translated to mean dwell. The Hebrew word for dwell is 'yashab' meaning to sit down together, to remain, to settle, to abide, to ease self, endure, and tarry. Our hearts long for community, yet our lives are so busy. Don't give up on building community... sometimes it just takes patience.

Thirdly, you want to **Serve**. God has blessed you with spiritual gifts, and He wants you to use them. If you don't know your spiritual gifts I would suggest taking a Spiritual Gifts Assessment. Lifeway has a great tool on their website[a]. Print it off and take it. I Peter 4:10NIV says, "Each of you should use whatever gift you have received to serve others, as faithful stewards of God's grace in its various forms." A great way to serve others is to get involved in ministry at your church. Let me insert this here so we are all on the same page – you can use your gifts outside of the four walls of the church, and serve others in numerous settings. Your gifts are to help build up the Kingdom of God, which makes them transferable, not stationary. For example, if you have the gift of 'help'; have a great presence, and a welcoming demeanor, serving with the hospitality committee could be your ministry. If you have the gift of 'administration', meaning you are great with numbers, and can be very discreet with personal information, then perhaps working with the finance team would be a great fit. If you are not sure of your gifts, that's okay. Ask a ministry leader what's available and start serving. The first ministry may not be your last ministry, but start somewhere, take the initiative and make it happen.

The last part of the process is **Share**, meaning share your faith. We all are held accountable to the Great

Commission, according to Matthew 28:19-20 NIV, "Therefore go and make disciples of all nations baptizing them in the name of the Father and of the Son and of the Holy Spirit, and teaching them to obey everything I have commanded you. And surely I am with you always, to the very end of the age." You may be shaking in your stilettos right about now. You may be thinking that you are not a missionary, evangelist, nor a preacher. You don't have to be, but you already know how to evangelize. How do I know? Think about a time you were excited about a new movie, a new restaurant, or new fashion trend. Did you jump at the first chance to share the opportunity with someone you love? It's human nature to be a great mouthpiece for what we are excited about. Since you are excited about your developing relationship with the Father you should tell someone else, right? Right. You don't need to know every verse in the bible to evangelize. Just tell them your testimony, and invite them to church. It's really that simple. The woman at the well did not know multiple verses. She had an encounter with Jesus at the well and she ran and told everyone she knew. I am putting here a great deal of this story here so you can understand how you can share your faith based on your encounter with Jesus. John 4: 7-30 (NIV) says:

> "When a Samaritan woman came to draw water, Jesus said to her, "Will you give me a drink?" (His disciples had gone into the town to buy food.) The Samaritan woman said to him, "You are a Jew and I am a Samaritan woman. How can you ask me for a drink?" (For Jews do not associate with Samaritans). Jesus

answered her, "If you knew the gift of God and who it is that asks you for a drink, you would have asked him and he would have given you living water."

"Sir," the woman said, "you have nothing to draw with and the well is deep. Where can you get this living water? Are you greater than our father Jacob, who gave us the well and drank from it himself, as did also his sons and his livestock?" Jesus answered, "Everyone who drinks this water will be thirsty again, but whoever drinks the water I give them will never thirst. Indeed, the water I give them will become in them a spring of water welling up to eternal life." The woman said to him, "Sir, give me this water so that I won't get thirsty and have to keep coming here to draw water." He told her, "Go, call your husband and come back." "I have no husband," she replied. Jesus said to her, "You are right when you say you have no husband. The fact is, you have had five husbands, and the man you now have is not your husband. What you have just said is quite true." "Sir," the woman said, "I can see that you are a prophet. Our ancestors worshiped on this mountain, but you Jews claim that the place where we must worship is in Jerusalem." "Woman," Jesus replied, "believe me, a time is coming when you will worship the Father neither on this mountain nor in Jerusalem. You Samaritans worship what you do not know; we worship what we do know, for salvation is from the Jews. Yet a time is coming and has now come when the true worshipers will worship the Father in the Spirit and in truth, for they

> are the kind of worshipers the Father seeks. God is spirit, and his worshipers must worship in the Spirit and in truth." The woman said, "I know that Messiah (called Christ) is coming. When he comes, he will explain everything to us." Then Jesus declared, "I, the one speaking to you—I am he." Just then his disciples returned and were surprised to find him talking with a woman. But no one asked, "What do you want?" or "Why are you talking with her?" Then, leaving her water jar, the woman went back to the town and said to the people, "Come, see a man who told me everything I ever did. Could this be the Messiah?" They came out of the town and made their way toward him."

Having an encounter with Jesus, who tells you things about yourself, makes you want to tell others about this Savior.

In the development phase, you start to experience numerous things and hopefully one of the experiences is love. Falling in love is such a great feeling. I remember when I fell in love with my boo (not the single moment, but the process.) Our relationship was established, but I had this strong desire to develop it. I wanted our relationship to be strong and unbreakable. I loved him! I was Jason's Girl (still am). That's what you will begin to experience as you develop your relationship with the Father. You are no longer [INSERT NAME], you are Daddy's Girl. A father and daughter's relationship is so special. If you have a great bond with your Earthly father, then you know what I am talking about. If you do not, then you can still experience it with your Heavenly

Father. You are HIS BABY GIRL, Daddy's Girl. There is a great song by Heartland titled "I Loved Her First." What a beautiful song that focuses on what a father really means to his daughter. Here are some of the lyrics:

> "I loved her first
> I held her first
> And a place in my heart will always be hers
> From the first breath she breathed
> When she first smiled at me
> I knew the love of a father runs deep
> And I prayed that she'd find you someday
> But it's still hard to give her away
> I loved her first."

Challenge:

Meditate – find a scripture regarding your situation and ponder on it daily until the answer comes to you. Study – go to a bookstore, and get resources (bibles, commentaries, books). Pray – don't hang up on God.

Examine your personal relationship with God. Be brutally honest with yourself. No matter what level you are on, there is still room to grow. Examples – just starting your walk: pick a time for you to commune with God daily (scripture and prayer) or increase commune time with God. The goal is to have an unbreakable personal relationship with our Father where you can call Him Abba---translated to mean Daddy/Papa. Find a church home, be consistent on Sunday's, join a life group/bible study group, serve in a ministry, and share your faith.

Daddy's Girl

Ebony's Corner:

When I wanted to get serious about loving and living for God I had to examine where I was. I really wanted a relationship, but wasn't sure how to get there, so I made sure that I immersed myself in Him. I didn't engross myself in a fanatical way, but I began to date Him by spending time with Him daily. I started slowly, with 5 to 10 minutes of reading the Word and prayer. It was hard at first, because I couldn't keep my concentration... and because I didn't think I was "feeling," "experiencing," or "seeing" anything. However, I knew that if I wanted to develop the relationship, then I had to be patient. Afterwhile, my husband and I joined a church and were able to get connected to a few couples. Those couples stood beside us, and walked with us in faith. I grew closer to a few ladies in the church, (more mature in the faith than me) and we intentionally set time aside to hang out together. We began to share life experiences, and open the Word of God to answer those questions and help solve the problems. Over time I became more and more excited about God's never ending love for me. One day my Pastor during my developmental stage, Dr. Addis Moore, had me be the reader of the scripture. Afterwards, he said something that has stuck with me to this day. Now, I'm somewhat a fast reader – not on purpose – and Dr. Moore stopped me mid-sentence and said, "Don't read the bible like a newspaper, but read it for what it is – a love letter addressed to you!" WOW! That stopped me in my tracks. God loved me so much that He breathed life, and put words into the hearts and spirits of those to write the doctrine all for ME. I love to receive love letters from my Jason... but the bible is

THEE best love letter written with me in mind. So that thought changed me, challenged me, encouraged me, and inspired me to sincerely BE the best daughter of Christ I could be.

Chapter Two

Purposed

Discover and Operate in Your God-Given Purpose

Chapter One began with 'Establishing and Developing a Personal Relationship with Christ' for a reason. I said that knowing the Creator of the Universe and the Savior of Mankind lends itself to knowing who you are. It's like meeting a person who has been adopted, regardless of the circumstances, often times they have a desire to know who their birth parents are. You may hear them say, "I need to know who I am;" almost like they feel incomplete until they learn about their birth family. The same goes with Christ - we feel incomplete until we know Him. Once we understand who He is, then you know (or begin to know) yourself. Then you come to this understanding of Ephesians 2:10 (AMP), "For we are God's [own] handiwork (His workmanship), recreated in Christ Jesus, [born anew] that we may do those good works which God predestined (planned beforehand) for us [taking paths which He prepared ahead of time], that we should walk in them [living the good life which He prearranged and made ready for us to live]." Handiwork is a masterpiece, a one of a kind. When you realize that out of the entire human race, God made only one you, then you can comprehend how you are the only one who is qualified to do what God created you to do. On the contrary, without Christ you lose those qualifications. Come on somebody! Girl, high five yourself.

Your purpose and the calling of every believer is to build the Kingdom of God, but each person has a different role in this project. God must and will reveal to you how to utilize your gifts and talents in His Kingdom work.

For clarification and understanding - gifts are different from talents. For example – a praise and worship leader's talent could be singing, while her gift is exhortation. Exhortation is a special empowerment from God to motivate people to do something. To see this at work listen to Tamela Mann's "Take Me To the King" or Kierra "KiKi" Sheard's "Indescribable". I want to fall out every time I hear these ladies sang. Yes, SANG. Have you ever heard two people sing the same gospel song, but one person gets you out of your seat with tears rolling down your face... while the other just makes you feel like you are at a concert? The difference? The gift at work versus the talent being on display.

So, you might be asking, "Well how do I discover my purpose, so that I can operate in it?" There are a couple of ways that I am going to highlight. I touched on joining a church in the first chapter but I will expound upon it in this chapter.

Embrace What Irritates You

My former Pastor, Dr. Addis Moore of Kalamazoo, Michigan, would say, "There was a problem in the Earth realm that activated your birth and your journey is to find the problem." Let's pause here. Let that quote sink in. Girl, that's so good, so let me repeat it. There was a problem in the Earth realm that activated your birth and your journey is to find the problem. Do you get it? You are special. You are one of a kind! There is no one else like you in all the Earth. Isn't that awesome and mind-boggling at the same time? Okay, let's jump back in. When there is a problem it, usually irritates you.

I was listening to Willie Moore Jr. one evening while driving in my car. (He's an inspirational speaker, actor, comedian, and radio host who landed a record deal with Universal Records after college singing Hip-Hop and R&B.) He often talks about how after his shows he would go to his room and read the bible while everyone else went to hang out. As he got more into the Word of God, the climate of the environment of the young people around began to bother him. He found his purpose by being so upset about this "lost generation" that he turned to gospel music. Willie Moore Jr. left secular music at the height of his career. Hold up! He left something that was good because he knew it wasn't great. Are you there? It feels good, looks good, smells good but it's not good for you because it is not the best for you! Somebody say Amen! He stopped complaining about it and acted. Ask yourself, "What gets me fired up?" or "What can I talk about all day?" Have you ever said, "Somebody needs to (you fill in the blank)?" There are three ways that you can get this figured out and I'll use passages from the bible to help illustrate this point.

One way to figure out what breaks your heart is if you **SEE THE PROBLEM.** In Matthew 9, we witness Jesus being moved with compassion based on what he saw. Matthew 9:35-38 NIV says, "Jesus went through all the towns and villages, teaching in their synagogues, proclaiming the good news of the kingdom and healing every disease and sickness. When he saw the crowds, he had compassion on them, because they were harassed and helpless, like sheep without a shepherd. Then he said to his disciples, 'The harvest is plentiful but the workers are few. Ask the Lord of the harvest, therefore, to send out workers into his harvest field.'" Jesus saw the people, and it broke His heart because they were harassed and helpless, like sheep without a shepherd. He was so moved that he took action – prayer. What have you seen that has broken your heart?

The second way to figure out what breaks your heart is if you **HEAR ABOUT THE PROBLEM.** Nehemiah was moved because he got word that the walls of Jerusalem were broken down and people were in exile. So Nehemiah 1:4-11 (NIV) says:

> "When I heard these things, I sat down and wept. For some days I mourned and fasted and prayed before the God of heaven. Then I said: "Lord, the God of heaven, the great and awesome God, who keeps his covenant of love with those who love him and keep his commandments, let your ear be attentive and your eyes open to hear the prayer your servant is praying before you day and night for your servants, the people of Israel. I confess the sins we Israelites, including myself and my father's family, have committed against you. We have acted very wickedly toward you. We have not obeyed the commands, decrees and laws you gave your servant Moses. "Remember the

> instruction you gave your servant Moses, saying, 'If you are unfaithful, I will scatter you among the nations, 9 but if you return to me and obey my commands, then even if your exiled people are at the farthest horizon, I will gather them from there and bring them to the place I have chosen as a dwelling for my Name.' "They are your servants and your people, whom you redeemed by your great strength and your mighty hand. Lord, let your ear be attentive to the prayer of this your servant and to the prayer of your servants who delight in revering your name. Give your servant success today by granting him favor in the presence of this man." I was cupbearer to the king."

Even though Nehemiah heard about the walls of Jerusalem being broken down, it still broke his heart so much so that he began to act – with prayer - so that he could be a part of the solution. So, what have you heard about that has pricked your heart?

Lastly, the third way to figure out what has broken your heart is if **YOU ARE THE PROBLEM.** I know we may not want to admit this, but sometimes we can be the problem or have the problem that is of concern. I love the Prophet Isaiah because he was very transparent in chapter six. Isaiah 6:5-8 NIV says:

> ""Woe to me!" I cried. "I am ruined! For I am a man of unclean lips, and I live among a people of unclean lips, and my eyes have seen the King, the Lord Almighty." Then one of the

> seraphim flew to me with a live coal in his hand, which he had taken with tongs from the altar. With it he touched my mouth and said, "See, this has touched your lips; your guilt is taken away and your sin atoned for." Then I heard the voice of the Lord saying, "Whom shall I send? And who will go for us?" And I said, "Here am I. Send me!'"

After seeing holiness and righteousness, Isaiah realized that he had a personal problem, and he dwelt amongst others that were dealing with the same thing. Once he repented, a clear path was made for the Lord to speak to him. As much as we may not want to deal with or recognize our issues, dealing with them can prove to be advantageous for you and for someone else. So, what can you honestly admit is a problem in your life that has shattered your heart? Figuring out the problem is the first step, but you may also need to ask yourself, "Is this bigger than me?" Plainly, can I do this on my own or does Jesus need to be in the driver's seat? Because we want to be in the driver's seat, we shortchange the Holy Spirit. Second Corinthians 5:7 says, "For we walk by faith and not by sight." Don't be afraid to jump right in and let the Holy Spirit guide you while you embrace what irritates you (we'll talk about the Holy Spirit later in the book). It always bothered me to see young women walking around not embracing their womanhood, and acting out of order because they did not understand who they really are. You don't act up when you know your name! My maiden name is Jackson, and where I'm from, that last name carried some weight and was synonymous with having it together. I knew better than to be in those streets acting a fool because I represented a slew of Jacksons. I realized that some young women were missing something, and I was the answer. Showing young women that they can lead a successful, God-centered life is part of my purpose. What irritates you? Get some passion behind it, and get going.

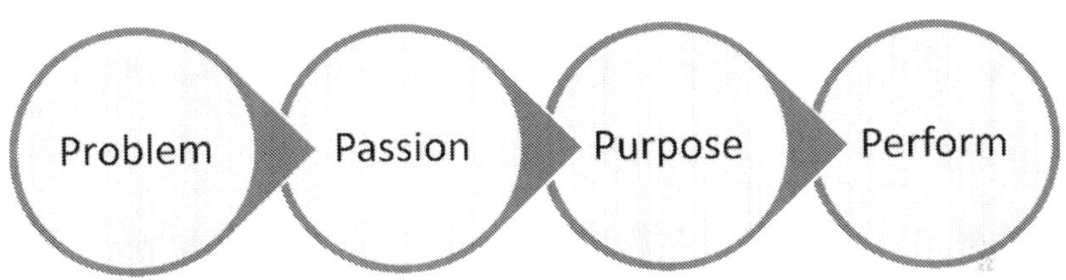

Get Equipped

Another way to discover and operate in your God-given purpose is through this verse: Ephesians 4:11-12 (AMP) says, "And His gifts were [varied; He Himself appointed and gave men to us] some to be apostles (special messengers), some prophets (inspired preachers and expounders), some evangelists (preachers of the Gospel, traveling missionaries), some pastors (shepherds of His flock) and teachers. His intention was the perfecting and the full equipping of the saints (His consecrated people), [that they should do] the work of ministering toward building up Christ's body (the church)." You may not be the apostle, prophet, evangelist, pastor, or teacher so you need to get equipped. How do you do that? Join a local assembly of believers – a church. Get under some training – worship service, bible study, classes, find a mature saint to be your mentor, and get equipped. To equip means to supply with the necessary items for a particular purpose or prepare (someone) mentally for a particular situation or task.

The Word of God will walk you into your purpose. Psalm 119:105 says, "Your word is a lamp to my feet and a light to my path." I love Theologian Matthew Henry's commentary[b] for this verse. It says in part:

> "The nature of the word of God, and the great intention of giving it to the world; it is a lamp and a light. It discovers to us, concerning God and ourselves, that which otherwise we could not have known. It is a lamp, which we may set up by us, and take into our hands for our own particular use. It must be not only a light to our eyes, to gratify them, and fill our heads with speculations, but a light to our feet and to our path, to direct us in the right ordering of our conversation, both in the choice of our way in general and in the particular steps we take in that way, that we may not take a false way nor a false step in the right way. We are then truly sensible of God's goodness to us in giving us such a lamp and light when we make it a guide to our feet, our path."

That is a mouth full, but in essence he's saying, the Word of God illuminates the path and highlights the next step. The fundamental truth; however, is there must be a consistent, forward motion on our part. Contrary to belief, most times, your purpose doesn't fall in your lap. We're "searching" for this BIG, miraculous thing; whereas, God wants us to obey that thing. Psalm 37:23 (AMP) says, "The steps of a [good] man are directed and established by the Lord when He delights in his way [and He busies Himself with his every step]." Our steps and our paths are directed and established by God. Let me give you a real, true, sho nuff example.

My husband, Reverend Jason "Pastor J" Robinson, is our Pastor but he didn't start there. In his early years, he didn't necessarily know his purpose, but he knew enough to get into the Word of God and sit under some biblical teaching. He wanted to get active in ministry, but didn't know where to begin so he was asked to be responsible for microphones and the screens, working on the sound board at church. The soundboard was positioned in the back of the church. Oftentimes, while he was doing his ministry assignment, he would see that the ushers needed help seating people. What was very critical for ushers was the importance of having men to greet other men. Pastor J discerned it wasn't necessarily about seating men, it was more than that, so his heart was pricked and he joined the Usher's Ministry. As he served as an usher, he would see people from the street come into the church, and noticed that because they didn't "understand" the Word, they didn't give the Word a chance to penetrate. Accordingly, he felt a burden on his heart to reach those individuals in their own comfort zone: the streets. He decided to join the Evangelism team, a platform that allowed him to both share the Gospel, and learn more about people's everyday struggles. It irritated him that people couldn't receive the Word due to so many other issues that needed to be addressed, first and foremost. He knew this was an issue that God was leading him to help solve in the church.

Later, he was introduced to the Stephens Ministry. Stephen Ministers are laypeople—Christian men and women—trained to provide one-on-one care to people experiencing a difficult time in life such as: grief, divorce, job loss, chronic or terminal illness, relocation, or separation due to military deployment. As he ministered and counseled life issues, he then could truly minister the Word. His diligence for the Word and his concern for people positioned him to participate in Teacher's Training. He became a Fulfillment Hour teacher, better known as a Sunday School instructor. Serving in Sunday School stirred up the preacher within Pastor J, resulting in his enrollment, training, licensure, and finally ordainment as a minister. Following his transition, we moved, joined another church, and eventually he became an Associate Minister (an assistant to the Pastor.) Those responsibilities and duties, along with God pricking his heart, led him to being a Church Planter (which is a minister that starts a new congregation where none previously exist) and Pastor. Pastor J, myself, and a handful of others launched Reach Church in Ypsilanti, Michigan in September 2014. Pastor J's purpose is to deliver the Word of God with clarity, relevance, and with the intention to have people do something differently. Whew! That was a lot! But the point here is when you get equipped, your purpose will ooze out of what you do. It becomes like stepping stones to elevate you to the next thing.

There is this terrific book called, *S.H.A.P.E.: Finding and Fulfilling Your Unique Purpose for Life*, by Erik Rees, a follow up book from Rick Warren's *Purpose Driven Life* ®, which new members receive at Reach Church. When they come to our New Members Luncheon we give them this book because we want them to get an understanding of their S.H.A.P.E. very early on so that they can start walking in their purpose. I highly recommend getting this book and diving in. [Remember, you are trying to get better, so any tools out there that will help in your growth process and becoming equipped should be a priority.] As I was surfing on the Internet I came across this awesome publisher's description[c] about this book and I want to put it here to entice you to GO GET THE BOOK:

> Now Erik Rees helps you discover God's unique purpose for your life based on the way God has shaped you. He made you marvelously unique for a reason. Tap into that reason and into the secrets of your own deeply personal makeup—the remarkable ensemble of passions, talents, experiences, temperament, and spiritual gifts that work together to make you who you are—and you'll discover the path to a life of unimagined purpose, impact, and fulfillment. In this eye-opening, empowering, and liberating book, Rees shows you how to uncover God's most powerful and effective means of advancing his kingdom on earth: your own irreplaceable, richly detailed personal design. Based on the purpose of ministry outlined in The Purpose Driven Life, this inspiring guidebook gives you the tools to: Unlock your God-given potential, Uncover your specific Kingdom Purpose, Unfold a kingdom plan for your life Filled with

> Scripture and real-life stories. S.H.A.P.E. presents a series of challenges that will guide you through the process of discovering your personal blend of Spiritual Gifts: A set of special abilities that God has given you to share his love and serve others. Heart: The special passions God has given you so that you can glorify him on earth. Abilities: The set of talents God gave you when you were born, which he also wants you to use to make an impact for him. Personality: The special way God wired you to navigate life and fulfill your unique Kingdom Purpose. Experiences: Those parts of your past, both positive and painful, which God intends to use in great ways. It's all here: insights that can change the way you look at yourself and how you live your life and practical guidance for applying them. Discover how to apply your amazing array of personal attributes in ways that bring confidence, freedom, clarity, and significance that can only come from your Creator.

Doesn't that get you excited?! What's awesome is that God made one of you and that your S.H.A.P.E. is different from everyone else's. Get going on taking your spiritual gifts assessment. Understand and embrace what irritates you. What breaks your heart? God has given us talents that allow us to grow His Kingdom. Isn't it great to know that your quirky personality is designed to help you go through and see life in a unique way and that uniqueness is designed to help someone else? Lastly, your experiences are designed to be a message for the masses. Yes, EVERY experience. The great, happy go lucky experiences, and yes my sweet sister, even the ones you don't want to talk about. The ones you wish would go away. The ones you don't want to think about anymore. Romans 8:28 AMP says, "And we know [with great confidence] that God [who is deeply concerned about us] causes all things to work together [as a plan] for good for those who love God, to those who are called according to His plan and purpose."

Discovering and operating in your purpose becomes a cycle. You discover your purpose, and then you operate in it. Then you discover something else, and you operate in that too. Like Nike says, "Just DO it." In this case, the DO is Discover and Operate. Angela Duckworth, author of "Grit: The Power of Passion and Perseverance" says, "Interests are not discovered through introspection. Instead, interests are triggered by interactions with the outside world". However, I believe we do need some introspection. Our introspection comes with being self-aware, and by communing and worshipping with our Father. External triggers are important as well. An external trigger could be seeing teenagers not having role models, and noticing that it bothers you. Another one could be a child not knowing how to express themselves in a positive manner. The external triggers can be embracing what irritates you and getting equipped in your local church. What else are you going to do to embrace the external triggers? S.H.A.P.E.

Challenge:

Embrace what irritates you. Obviously, some things may not be for you, but discern if you are the answer to the problem. Lead with passion to get it done. Much like you get trained for a new job, it is important to get trained as a Kingdom builder. Take knowing your purpose in life seriously and do the proper steps to discover and operate in it.

Ebony's Corner:

As a young child, I was always questioned why my life mattered. Seriously, I did. I can remember as a child wondering why I was born and what I was supposed to do as an adult. I was thinking in terms of a career, not necessarily a Kingdom focus. As I got older, that desire to learn my purpose grew immensely. My curiosity was not about my career, (well that too) but more of the desire to ascertain the reason God placed me on this earth. I seriously wanted to know! I realized that me finding my purpose would squelch the feeling that I was 'missing something'. Notice I said something, not someone! Remember my sister no one can complete you! You are complete in Christ (Colossians 2:10). I hope that parenthetical statement helped you. What was I missing? I couldn't put my finger on it. But I knew who would direct me to get there. My loving Father would order my steps as I sought to get equipped. I was consistent in worship service, prayer service, bible study, Sunday school, and tithing. I believed that my obedience would yield results - most specifically, finding my role in God's story. I no longer wanted to be the star of the show. I wanted to be a supporting role for God. My ability to embrace what broke my heart with integrity and joy would prove to be relevant for some. I realized that my S.H.A.P.E. might not be for everyone. I mean seriously, there are over 7 billion people in the world and my purpose may not be for everyone, but I was created to meet someone's need and I had a hunger and passion to do that. I honestly believe that my purpose is to help people know who they are in Christ in a relevant way. My talents and abilities have put me in other places to do other things, but I know what the main thing is, and I intend to keep the main thing the main thing.

Chapter Three

Unleashed

Understands and Unleashes the Power that Resides in Her

Welcome to Chapter Three. You are moving along, and my prayer is that you are learning and applying what you've learned. You may be familiar with the popular saying, "Knowledge is Power." While that is true, if you don't do something with the knowledge then it is null and void. So please my dear sister, apply what you are reading. Take this information and, put feet to it.

I'm excited about this chapter. You are making your way through this process! You have established and developed a relationship with the Father. Because of that relationship, you have discovered and are operating in your God-given purpose. Hopefully you understand that the purpose God has given you is bigger than you, therefore you need the Holy Spirit's power to complete it. This chapter will help you understand and unleash the power that resides in you (the Holy Spirit.)

Understand the Power

The word power sounds so good, right? Who doesn't want power? It's okay to raise your hand, I will not judge you. In this context you may be wondering – what is this power and how can I get it? The power I'm speaking of comes if you are saved and have confessed Romans 10:9 (AMP), "Because if you acknowledge and confess with your lips that Jesus is Lord and in your heart believe (adhere to, trust in, and rely on the truth) that God raised Him from the dead, you will be saved." The moment you accept Jesus Christ as your Lord and Savior, the Holy Spirit takes up residence in your heart, and the power is in you. The problem is that it is just lying there dormant – inactive because you may not understand the power. The power is the Holy Spirit. Don't freak out, turn on all your lights, or close this book- there is nothing scary about the Holy Spirit. The Holy Spirit is part of the trinity – the Father, Son, and the Holy Spirit. The Holy Spirit is not an "it", the spirit is a person. John 14:15-17 (AMP) states, "If you [really] love Me, you will keep (obey) My commands. And I will ask the Father, and He will give you another Comforter (Counselor, Helper, Intercessor, Advocate, Strengthener, and Standby), that He may remain with you forever—The Spirit of Truth, Whom the world cannot receive (welcome, take to its heart), because it does not see Him or know and recognize Him. But you know and recognize Him, for He lives with you [constantly] and will be in you."

The Holy Spirit has many purposes, but I will highlight just a few.

The Holy Spirit is a teacher and helps us to remember His Word. Have you ever found yourself in a position where you were about to argue with someone at work or school and the Holy Spirit "snatched you up?" He may have brought to your remembrance Proverbs 24:6 (NIV), which says, "Do not answer a fool according to his folly, or you yourself will be just like him." That's good, because you will not waste your time trying to prove your point when the person is foolish and is not concerned with truth. John 14:26 (AMP) says, "But the Comforter (Counselor, Helper, Intercessor, Advocate, Strengthener, Standby), the Holy Spirit, Whom the Father will send in My name [in My place, to represent Me and act on My behalf], He will teach you all things. And He will cause you to recall (will remind you of, bring to your remembrance) everything I have told you." He empowers us to be witnesses. Acts 1:8 (AMP) says, "But you shall receive power (ability, efficiency, and might) when the Holy Spirit has come upon you, and you shall be My witnesses in Jerusalem and all Judea and Samaria and to the ends (the very bounds) of the earth." The Holy Spirit will give you the boldness and courage to go and be a witness for Him in all parts of the world. What I want you to understand is, the Holy Spirit is in us to be our GPS. Instead of Global Positioning System, it is our Godly Positioning System. The system tells you where you are located, where your next destination is, and the process to get there. Proverbs 3:5-6 (NIV) is one of my favorite verses which says, "Trust in the Lord with all your heart and lean not on your own understanding; in all your ways submit to him, and he will make your paths straight." The GPS is only useful when the owner is using it. That was good girl! Did you catch it? Your Godly Positioning System – the Holy Spirit – is only useful when the owner – you – uses it. Get it out girl! Use it girl! Get your GPS out.

Unleash the Power

You may be wondering why I'm saying unleash. The Holy Spirit is definitely not an untamed animal. But, I will say that we have tied, chained, and bound the Holy Spirit in a spiritual sense. Picture the Holy Spirit tied up to a pole wishing that He could be free to help you. Did you picture that? We have not allowed the Holy Spirit to function the way that Jesus believed to be sincerely important. So the pressing question is, "how do I unleash the spirit?" In the first chapter, I talked about how we make things complicated when Jesus is saying it is simple. The same concept applies here as well. It is not that complicated, my sweet friend. We will discuss two ways to unleash the Holy Spirit.

The first answer lies in being trusting enough to be led. This is going to be a doozy, so buckle up lady- here we go! Most of us only trust ourselves. Yikes! The word trust can be a cuss word in some of our worlds, right? But, this is so critical to unleash the Holy Spirit. Have you ever seen those trust exercises where Person A is the guide, and Person B has on a blindfold? They are on an obstacle course and Person A must get Person B through it. The problem with the situation is that Person B has seen the course and is freaking out. Why are they freaking out? Because they remembered how jacked up the course was. So, before they put the blindfold on they are trying to memorize where the obstacles are, the turns, the pitfalls, the easy spots, etc. Never once (most times) did Person B say or think, "I'm so glad Person A is my guide; I will gladly put on my blindfold." Nope not at all! They are yelling, going the opposite direction, and all out quitting. Person A is so frustrated because they see the course and they are confident with the outcome, but they need Person B to simply trust. This next scripture has been mentioned before, but it's so good that I had to share it again in this section. (Hint, Hint – this means write this down, take a picture, burn it in your memory, learn it like you are going to recite this as your Easter speech). Proverbs 3:5-6 (AMP) says, "Lean on, trust in, and be confident in the Lord with all your heart and mind and do not rely on your own insight or understanding. In all your ways know, recognize, and acknowledge Him, and He will direct and make straight and plain your paths." More often than not, we tell the Holy Spirit "I got this" and "please have several seats!" Basically, we tell the Holy Spirit to be quiet. Now check this out - this is so interesting: If you don't study the Word, then when a problem comes up there is nothing in you for the Holy Spirit to recall to memory. You can't know your purpose in life if you have not allowed the Holy Spirit to guide you in that process. God gives the gifts. You can't expect to have any power if you have the Holy Spirit on "break." I know I'm on somebody's street! I did not mean to bust your bubble. But my dear sister, you must learn how to trust. How do you learn how to do that? Well, I learned an acronym a long time ago from Pastor Nathan Johnson of Detroit, Michigan:

T.R.U.S.T. Totally Relying (Resting) Upon The Scriptures Truth. Not halfway trusting, but totally trusting. The word relying can be translated as "leaning on". You know when you lean on your friend and all of your body's weight is on them and they are ready to fall over? You need to have that type of leaning and relying on the Word of God. Let me stress this - The TRUTH, not some made up information. T.R.U.S.T. Write that down, put that in your phone's notes, and bring that up daily. The Word is not inconsistent and does not change its mind. Hebrews 13:8 (NIV) says, "Jesus Christ is the same yesterday and today and forever." I don't know about you, but I love the way that scripture sounds! You must admit that as much as you care for your loved ones, they can be inconsistent at times. We serve a great God who NEVER changes unlike our parents, siblings, or friends. If that isn't good news, I don't know what is. Trust the Holy Spirit!

Secondly, it is essential to be aware and alert. When the Holy Spirit says go, you go. When the Holy Spirit says stop, you stop. My son Solomon goes to occupational therapy, and one of the activities his therapist does with him involves tracing straight and curved lines. Each line is vertical so, at the bottom of the line there is a green light and at the top of the line, a red light. When he gets started with the lines, the Occupational Therapist will say, "Green means go and read means stop." Solomon has been programmed enough to listen for her voice, and to follow her directions. What is interesting is that despite the background noise, he is able to discern her voice, and still follow her directions successfully. He can do this because he has spent enough time with her to recognize her voice. Just like

Solomon, it is key to spend time with the Holy Spirit so you can recognize His voice. John 10:27 (NIV) says, "My sheep listen to my voice, I know them, and they follow me." We recognize the voices of those we spend time with. My mother could have been on the other side of the room, but when she called my name I knew it was her. I knew my mother's laugh, cough, and movements. Just like I know my mom's voice, we should know His voice. Therefore, be aware and alert for the voice to speak. You many not hear the voice audibly, so you want to be alert to the signs that are given through people and situations. God spoke from a burning bush (Exodus 3:2 (NIV) –"There the angel of the Lord appeared to him in flames of fire from within a bush. Moses saw that though the bush was on fire it did not burn up."), through people (Acts 9:17 (NIV) –"Then Ananias went to the house and entered it. Placing his hands on Saul, he said, "Brother Saul, the Lord—Jesus, who appeared to you on the road as you were coming here—has sent me so that you may see again and be filled with the Holy Spirit."), and His presence, which spoke volumes in the fiery furnace (Daniel 3:25 (NIV) – "He said, 'Look! I see four men walking around in the fire, unbound and unharmed, and the fourth looks like a son of the gods.'"). It's time for the Holy Spirit to rise and be the leader of your life. Unchain the Holy Spirit. Unleash the Holy Spirit my beautiful sister. Do it now, do not delay.

There are two definitions of power that work for our context that I want to get into your spirit. The first one is, "the ability to do something or act in a particular way". You have the ability. It is in you! You can do it! You can act kind, sisterly, powerful, and humble. You can do this! Power is also defined as, "the capacity or ability to direct or influence the behavior of others or the course of events". I love this definition because it shows us that we are influential. Stop saying that no one listens to you, or that you do not have leadership qualities. Girl! If you can direct or influence someone to go to the movies, buy dinner, or buy a dress, then you have the capacity to influence them to learn more and love on Jesus Christ. We are very powerful people, we just don't know it. You are powerful! You have just been too timid to use that power. Girl, get you some courage juice and drink away. You have been endowed with power. Let me hip you to this verse: Matthew 16:19 (NKJV), "And I will give you the keys of the kingdom of heaven, and whatever you bind on earth will be bound in heaven, and whatever you loose on earth will be loosed in heaven." When I was first introduced to this verse I didn't understand it. Well, I understood it, but I'm not sure if I truly *received* it. Just so we are on the same page, I want to provide some meaning of this verse. When a city or society is incorporated, officers are appointed and empowered to act for the good of the people in said city. A city without government is full of chaos and proves to be unsafe and hazardous. The government of the church is expressed in this verse by the delivering of the keys, which bring about a power to bind and loose. The power in this verse speaks to a spiritual power; it is a power pertaining to the kingdom of heaven, a power to bind and loose, that is to shut and open. Ladies, you have keys! If that isn't power, I don't know what is. When you have keys to a house, car, office, or building – you have the power to allow people in or not. We can tell situations in our lives, "you are improper and you have to go", or, "it is so" and it must be.

The Holy Spirit is there to guide you. He is your Comforter, Counselor, Helper, Intercessor, Advocate, Strengthener, and Standby. The Holy Spirit is no wimp and has given us access to mighty power. When you truly understand the purpose of the Holy Spirit then you will have no problem unleashing Him in your life.

Challenge:

Do some research on the Holy Spirit. Come to a better understanding of the Holy Spirit's purpose in your life specifically, guiding you to operate in your God-given purpose.

Take the chains off the Holy Spirit, and allow Him to lead and guide you. If you have trust issues, then it is time to empower yourself to erase those concerns! The Holy Spirit is your friend, so stop hanging your friend out to dry.

Ebony's Corner:

As a little girl I was spooked any time I heard the word 'spirits'. I just wanted to take off running! However, when I heard about the Holy Spirit, I wasn't spooked per say, but I was still unsure of what it was all about. Some of my friends described it as being something that makes you jump, scream, cry, shout, or run. In all seriousness, I did not "want it" if it was going to make me do all of that. Now, I have come to understand that that is not all the Holy Spirit does. Yes, the

Holy Spirit may have you jump, scream, cry, shout, or run, but there is so much more. I recognize that the Holy Spirit helps me, guides me, teaches me, and protects me. When I understood the Holy Spirit's purpose, I then embraced the importance it had in my life. I have learned to move out of the way, and allow the Holy Spirit to do His job. I no longer wanted to move in life on my own. I didn't want to flow through life hoping I would make it to my destination. I needed a guide to help me navigate through dangers, both seen and unseen (my grandmother and 'em use to say that). I needed an advocate on my behalf. I am so grateful that I saw past my wacky self, got off my high horse, and trusted the Holy Spirit to have my back. I will admit, it can be tough at times to fully let go, but in those tight-fisted moments I remind myself that the Holy Spirit was designed with me in mind. Jeremiah 29:11 (NKJV) says, "For I know the thoughts that I think toward you, says the Lord, thoughts of peace and not of evil, to give you a future and a hope." For me to get to the future and hope, I need to unleash the Holy Spirit... and I vow to make that happen.

Chapter Four

Maximize

Live and Maximize an Abundant Life

I used to run track in high school and college. Of all the various events, my favorite races were the relays, especially the 4x100m. In the 4x100m, four people run 100 meters each to get back to the start/finish line, each person playing an integral part of the relay team. In an article[d] blogged by Dennis Best, a retired Track and Field Coach from Coal City, Illinois High School called, "Exploiting your 4x100 meter Relay Personnel," the writer discusses the importance of each member of a relay team. The first runner must be good in the blocks, run the curve well, exchange the baton well, and is typically the 1st or 2nd fastest runner. The second runner is usually the 3rd or 4th fastest runner, good with the baton, and a good spot for the taller runner because of the straightway. The third runner is usually the 3rd or 4th fastest, good curve runner, disciplined in the exchange zone (tension and excitement will be building at this stage), and competitive; a good position for the shorter runner because of the acceleration around the curve. But that fourth runner - anchor leg - is special. This runner is usually the 1st or 2nd fastest runner on the team, disciplined in the exchange zone (tension and excitement will be at its peak at the exchange), mentally tough, enjoys running people down, and competitive. This chapter is the fourth runner – the anchor leg. This chapter will take it to the house. However, this chapter is only good if you can keep pace, be disciplined, exhibit mental toughness, enjoy an adventure, and are spirited. This is like taking all that you have learned, and turning it up a few notches. So, let's get this baton to the finish line.

Live An Abundant Life

What does an abundant life mean to you? Seriously, answer the question. I'll wait... I'll let the thinking music being to play...

You got it? Okay! Webster's Dictionary defines the word abundant as, "marked by great plenty and amply supplied". Essentially my sister, you can live a life that is plenty and amply supplied, a life that is prosperous and more than enough. That sounds awesome, doesn't it? I think I can assume that everyone wants to live that type of life. Now, some definitions may be different and skewed by the world's standard of what that is. By the world's standards, abundance could mean luxury vehicles, exquisite, massive homes, name brand everything, or more money in the bank account than the average person. This picture represents someone who can "ball out of control." However, I'm speaking of a life that God wants us to live. Mark 10:29-30 (NKJV) says, "So Jesus answered and said, 'Assuredly, I say to you, there is no one who has left house or brothers or sisters or father or mother or wife or children or lands, for My sake and the gospel's, who shall not receive a hundredfold now in this time—houses and brothers and sisters and mothers and children and lands, with persecutions—and in the age to come, eternal life'". What is so great about this verse is that Jesus gets that when we follow Him, we can suffer great loss. Jesus talks about the losses. He brings up houses first and land last as if to make a point. Houses and land represents worldly abundance and wealth. Sandwiched between those two, Jesus highlights relationships. To forsake mother, father, sister, or brother can be extremely hard. Seriously, could you do that? But the Word says that the advantage of doing those things is great. God gave Job double for his trouble (Job 42:10 (NIV), "After Job prayed for his friends, the Lord restored his fortunes and gave him twice as much as he had before") but for you (and I) we get a hundredfold. A hundredfold is a hundred times as much or as many, that sounds like an abundant life to me! Amen, Sister! However, remember I told you earlier that you would experience trouble? It was just mentioned in this verse, in the form of persecution. The persecution and trouble come along with the blessing as shown in the verse. So buckle up, because there will be drama in your life, BUT the promises of God should yield supernatural faith and confidence. Thankfully, the verse hasn't ended yet - there is more! We get the opportunity to live an abundant life on Earth, and then we get to experience eternal life in the hereafter. To experience eternal life you have to accept the sweetness of salvation. One more time for good measure: Romans 10:9 (NIV) says, "If you declare with your mouth, "Jesus is Lord," and believe in your heart that God raised him from the dead, you will be saved." I want to share three points that can enable you to live an abundant life. Get ready, grab your paper and pens, and read!

To live an abundant life first you need to have an abundant mentality. That's already good, right? A lot of us live with a scarcity mentality. A scarcity mentality believes the glass is half empty. This thinking is pessimistic, showing a lack of hope for the future, or expecting bad things to happen. You know? Stinking Thinking! Have you been around that type of person who sees the bad and lack in everything? You don't know that person? Is it you? Proverbs 18:21 says, "Death and life are in the power of the tongue." A person can do a great deal with that small member of the body. It can do an enormous amount of hurt, or an enormous amount of good. Just to push this point further, there is another set of verses that I want you to keep on your hip. James 3:3-7 (AMP) says:

> "Now if we put bits into the horses' mouths to make them obey us, we guide their whole body as well. And look at the ships. Even though they are so large and are driven by strong winds, they are still directed by a very small rudder wherever the impulse of the helmsman determines. In the same sense, the tongue is small part of the body, and yet it boasts of great things. See [by comparison] how great a forest is set on fire by a small spark! And the tongue is [in a sense] a fire, the very world of injustice and unrighteousness; the tongue is set among our members as that which contaminates the

> entire body, and sets on fire the course of our life [the cycle of man's existence], and is itself set on fire by hell."

Hopefully you got it! That small member – the tongue – can you mess you up if you are not careful. The tongue can set some things, situations, and relationships on fire when we do not practice self-discipline. A person with an abundant mentality will speak life, while a person with a scarcity mentality will speak death. Sometimes the death talk is done unintentionally because it is just the "normal talk". Unfortunately, we have conditioned ourselves with negative, toxic relationships and behaviors so much that it has become routine. Please inspect this behavior in your own life. Even if you feel like a failure, you must remember that you are more than a conqueror (Romans 8:37 (NSAB) – "But in all these things we overwhelmingly conquer through Him who loved us"). Even if you don't have everything you want please remember that God will supply all your needs (Philippians 4:19 (NASB) – "And my God will supply all your needs according to His riches in glory in Christ Jesus.") When you have an abundant mentality – you walk differently, talk differently, and view the situation differently. Have you ever watched the Food Network Show, *Chopped*? This show is a competition of chefs to see who can make the best appetizer, entrée, or desert using ingredients from the mystery basket that may not be the best, flavorful, appealing, or complementary. I am no means a chef... far from it. I can make my way around the kitchen, but no one is asking me to do a cooking show, nor dying to get a hold of my recipes. I'm just saying – I know my strengths and weaknesses (LOL!) If I were on Chopped I would fail miserably because I would look at those ingredients feeling hopeless. I would not know how to put a composed dish on the plate that comprised of jicama, duck breast, and cactus pears. I've never even seen or tasted two out of the three! Whereas, a chef would come alive, and make a masterful dish because their mindset is of abundance and positivity. They can look at the mystery basket ingredients as not just odd ingredients, but as a masterful dish that is able to please the judges in multiple ways. They're able to please the judges' senses as they see the beautiful colors, and smell the aroma whether it is sweet, salty, or spicy. Then, they awaken their taste buds as they taste and feel the food in their mouths. Just like those Master Chefs, you too have the ability to make the most of every situation. Change your stinking thinking today! Do it now, do not delay. My sister, it is a necessity to have a mentality of abundance.

Secondly, you must be content to live an abundant life. Philippians 4:11 tells us, "Not that I am implying that I was in any personal want, for I have learned how to be content (satisfied to the point where I am not disturbed or disquieted) in whatever state I am." Ladies, I'll keep it one hundred... that can be tough at times. Right? Your circle of friends may have more, so they can do more. Then comes the desire to keep up – getting caught up in risky behaviors (credit cards, revealing clothing (don't get me wrong we can be cute but we don't have to show everything to do so)), wanting the next baller, and we can go on and on. Even if we admire what others have, we don't have to have the attitude of jealousy, envy, or anger and belief that you will never have anything, nor do we have to choose to settle. Oh my, that nasty S Word.

Now settling and being content are two different things. I don't want you to read contentment, but walk away with settling. Settling is giving up on having something of value for something less than desired. Whereas, contentment is saying – I'm satisfied in my current situation because I know the Father owns the cattle on a thousand hills, (Psalm 50:10) and I'm His daughter. It's totally fine to have goals and want to reach them, and not be satisfied until reaching them. The difference is being discontent about not reaching the goal, versus being discontent about your current situation, yet doing nothing about it. Choose contentment today.

Finally, to live an abundant life you should start your day off correctly. My dear sister, only you can define how your day will go. Have you ever gotten up earlier than your usual time, and spent some quality time with God? Didn't your day seem different? You still may have had some problems, but your perspective on the problem was different, your feelings changed about the problem, and your reaction to the problem was calmer, more level headed. It's so important to wake up twice in the morning – physically and spiritually. Push yourself to not allow the social media platforms to be your first activity when you wake up in the morning. It is so important for you to guard your heart and mind. I'm not saying you should not be on social media, watch news outlets, or talk to people, but you want to be careful of what enters in your heart, soul, and mind. To provide some clarity, I want to emphasize my point with these verses: Luke 11:34-36 (AMP) says, "The eye is the lamp of your body. When your eye is clear [spiritually perceptive, focused on God], your whole body also is full of light [benefiting from God's precepts]. But when it is bad [spiritually blind], your body also is full of darkness [devoid of God's word]. Be careful, therefore, that the light that is in you is not darkness. So if your whole body is illuminated, with no dark part, it will be entirely bright [with light], as when the lamp gives you light with its bright rays." When you are spiritually sharp, keeping your focus on Christ, especially when making decisions, then there are benefits because of this focus and obedience. When you are opposite – unspiritual, having the focus to be on things not of Christ, then there are consequences. Making sense? Let me provide another passage of scripture – this is long one but a great one. Proverbs 2:2-12 (AMP) says:

> "So that your ear is attentive to [skillful and godly] wisdom, And apply your heart to understanding [seeking it conscientiously and striving for it eagerly]; Yes, if you cry out for insight, And lift up your voice for understanding; If you seek skillful and godly wisdom as you would silver And search for her as you would hidden treasures; Then you will understand the [reverent] fear of the Lord [that is, worshiping Him and regarding Him as truly awesome] And discover the knowledge of God. For the Lord gives [skillful and godly] wisdom; From His mouth come knowledge and understanding. He stores away sound wisdom for the righteous [those who are in right standing with Him]; He is a shield to those who

> walk in integrity [those of honorable character and moral courage], He guards the paths of justice; And He preserves the way of His saints (believers). Then you will understand righteousness and justice [in every circumstance] And integrity and every good path. For [skillful and godly] wisdom will enter your heart And knowledge will be pleasant to your soul. Discretion will watch over you, Understanding and discernment will guard you, to keep you from the way of evil and the evil man, from the man who speaks perverse things."

First, it is critical that you have the desire to be wise. From a biblical definition, wisdom is knowing and doing what is right. It is seeing things from God's perspective, and then responding to it according to biblical principles that you have learned. So these verses would strongly suggest to us that we should seek knowledge and understanding from God. That is not to say we can't learn from other outlets in moderation, but we want to be mindful of everything we consume. So, that question remains - How should you start your day? Go back to the beginning of the book – study, meditate, and pray. Study the Word, meditate on the Word, and pray to God using the Word. Jesus gives us a great example of these actions in Mark 1:35 NIV which says, "Very early in the morning, while it was still dark, Jesus got up, left the house and went off to a solitary place, where he prayed." Please note that Jesus, even while on Earth, was God, but He was also man. So Jesus, the man, gave us a Godly principle to model after. The principle here is to seek God before your day gets started. Communing with the

Father will provide clarity and direction for the day. You can get some questions answered on how to deal with a situation before you even walk out of the door. If you continue to read in Mark Chapter One, you will notice after the prayer that the disciples wanted him to continue His work in Capernaum, but Jesus thought it best to move on to other villages to do His work. Things were going wonderfully in Capernaum, why the need to move? Jesus' mission was for the nations, and not just a certain area. I also connect His prayer to His path for the day. Life was great in Capernaum. He was healing. He was popular, but it was time move along. This should further highlight the importance of seeking God first, early in the morning, to start your day off right.

Maximize an Abundant Life

Girl! I know you have the desire to live an abundant life. Right? I hope so. Now it is time to maximize that abundant life. The word maximize has several definitions, but for our purposes I want to use one which says, "to make the best use of". So how do we make the best use of our time, talents, gifts, and treasures?

I believe a wonderful way to maximize an abundant life is to prepare for opportunities. There is a famous Latin motto "Carpe Diem" which means to "Seize the Day." This concept's literal meaning is to take ahold of what is presented before you. I love this meaning because for me it gives a great illustration. I think of a person "taking a hold" of their day, and doing something with it. This person is saying that I am fully responsible and accountable for what my day, my week, my year, my life will look like, because I have decided to take action. Is that you my sister? Are you willing, wanting, desiring to "Carpe Diem?" Will you be accountable for what your day, week, year, and life looks like? Will you be responsible for taking action in your life? I hope you said yes to all of those questions, because life is so short.

Depending upon what data you view, the average life expectancy is reported differently. The Centers for Disease Control and Prevention's National Center for Health Statistics reports the current life expectancy is only 78.8 years old [e]. It seems like a long time, but time flies by. It's important to manage your time and view time as a hot commodity. Have you ever experienced a loved one passing away unexpectedly? One day they were living – happy, jovial, and full of life – and the next day they were gone. They had so many plans, but did not get the opportunity to fulfill them. I have heard this quote in numerous variations, but Motivational Speaker Les Brown says, "The graveyard is the richest place on earth, because it is here that you will find all the hopes and dreams that were never fulfilled, the books that were never written, the songs that were never sung, the inventions that were never shared, the cures that were never discovered, all because someone was too afraid to take that first step, keep with the problem, or determined to carry out their dream." Don't let this happen to you. You can prevent adding riches to the graveyard by preparing for opportunities. The opportunities will come, but you must be ready. I love this scripture because it puts things into perspective - James 4:14 (AMP) says, "Yet you do not know [the least thing] about what may happen tomorrow. What is the nature of your life? You are [really] but a wisp of vapor (a puff of smoke, a mist) that is visible for a little while and then disappears [into thin air]." James wrote that scripture as a warning about boasting, but we can apply the same principle here regarding not being prepared. James is literally saying that we have no idea what will happen tomorrow. That sounds like a great reason to seize the day. Life is short, frail, and uncertain, and these facts alone should provide the passion to get prepared. How do you prepare? Let's think back to chapter two – Purposed: Discover and Operate in Your God-Given Purpose. Do you recollect that chapter? Look through your notes. Get to flipping! Okay, just for you I will give a quick reminder and overview. Recall, you are to embrace what irritates you. There are three ways that you can get this figured out. One way to figure out what breaks your heart is if you SEE THE PROBLEM. We looked at *Matthew 9:35-38* for that point. Another way is to HEAR ABOUT THE PROBLEM. With this point we walked through *Nehemiah 1:4-11*. Lastly, a way to figure out what breaks your heart is if YOU ARE THE PROBLEM. To understand this point we observed the Prophet Isaiah in *Isaiah 6:5-8*. Also in that chapter we discussed the importance of getting equipped. I need you (you actually need yourself) to get in a bible based church that will teach you the Word of God, and show you how to apply the Word in your life. Remember, the bible has all of the answers, and you do not want to fail an open book test. So as you are discovering, your gifts will be revealed to you, which will then allow you to operate in them so that the Kingdom of God will be advanced. Proverbs 18:16

(NKJV) says, "A man's gift makes room for him and brings him before great men." That should be exciting! Why? You don't have to scheme, connive, or manipulate your gifts, because they alone will bring you to great men. Your gifts will allow you to meet the right people at the right time. Stop hating on other people. D(iscover) O(perate) YOU!

Grammy nominated singer, songwriter, actor, author, and more - Tyrese Gibson, was first discovered from a Coca Cola commercial. He rode a bus singing that famous line, "Always Coca-Cola." Before his big break, he had been preparing himself. What did he do? I'm sure he surrounded himself around experts in that area, asked for mentors to help guide him, took vocal lessons, and protected his voice by doing vocal exercises. He did all of that and probably more, so that when the opportunity arose he was ready to go. What do you desire to do? What was revealed to you when you discovered your God-given purpose? What breaks your heart? If someone came up to you today and said, "Let's do it!" would you be ready? Would you be ready for your own talk show? Would you be ready for your own fashion show? Would you be ready to launch that business? Would you be ready to finish the paperwork to start your non-profit? Would you be ready? Do you have a consistent work ethic when no else is watching? Know your gift(s), strengths, and weaknesses, develop your skills, and be alert. Seize the day! Be and stay prepared for the opportunities -- they will come.

The second way to maximize an abundant life is to become a master builder. A master builder is a person who is skilled in the art of building. You know building – the process of making structures by putting together materials. In the construction business there are Certified Master Builders. These individuals must meet strict requirements that demonstrate that this person is integral, an excellent service provider, and stable. A Certified Master Builder is required to complete a certain number of continuing education credit hours, which validate that they are keeping up with the latest information that will allow them to stay relevant and innovative as a CMB. So a Master Builder doesn't just lay a brick, they are creating something that has the ability to have longevity. They see more than just brick and mud, they see a solid building that is strong and can stand the test of time. Let's look at this passage of scripture found in 1 Corinthians 3:10-17 (NIV):

> "By the grace God has given me, I laid a foundation as a wise builder, and someone else is building on it. But each one should build with care. For no one can lay any foundation other than the one already laid, which is Jesus Christ. If anyone builds on this foundation using gold, silver, costly stones, wood, hay or straw, their work will be shown for what it is, because the Day will bring it to light. It will be revealed with fire, and the fire will test the quality of each person's work. If what has been built survives, the builder will receive a reward. If it is burned up, the builder will suffer loss but yet will be saved—even though only as one escaping through the flames. Don't you know that you yourselves are God's temple and that God's Spirit dwells in your midst? If

> anyone destroys God's temple, God will destroy that person; for God's temple is sacred, and you together are that temple."

As you are building, please make sure my dear sister, that Jesus Christ is your solid foundation. That is one of the reasons I stressed the importance of establishing and developing a relationship with Him. The foundation has to be firm for the house to be stable. Answer this question; Is He your firm foundation? Another characteristic of a Master Builder is their ability to "see" the finished product from the outset. I am suggesting that they have vision. Vision meaning, they have keen sight and observation. Maybe a practical way to understand it is that vision is the bridge between the present and the future. Vision allows you to keep pushing when your present may be bringing hardships. Proverbs 29:18 KJV says, "Where there is no vision, the people perish: but he that keepeth the law, happy is he." Not having a vision (which entails the Word of God) brings about chaos because no direction or instruction is clearly defined. I love this verse that is in Habakkuk (say that word a few times!) 2:2-3 because it gives us some great directives: "Then the Lord answered me and said: "Write the vision and make it plain on tablets, that he may run who reads it. For the vision is yet for an appointed time; but at the end it will speak, and it will not lie. Though it tarries, wait for it; because it will surely come, it will not tarry." In this verse it highlights the importance of having a vision. Write down the vision and make it simple. Have you head of the acronym K.I.S.S.? It means Keep It Simple St@pid. I am not a big fan of the last word, but you get the point. The verse tells you to run with it. Does that sound like 'Carpe Diem'? It does to me. The materialization of the vision is for a certain time. Your time is coming my dear Sister – keep going, do not quit. Even though it may seem to be taking too long, note in your heart and soul that it will happen. Have you heard that patience is a virtue? I heard that many times as a young woman, but I wasn't sure what it meant until I looked it up. That concept means the ability to wait for something without getting upset displays a great and valuable characteristic in that person. I have seen numerous examples of people being patient, and in particular being a master builder. Again, a master builder should be able to see what they have, and build upon it. For example, I love Kierra "KiKi" Sheard. She is the daughter of Bishop J. Drew, Pastor of Greater Emmanuel Institutional COGIC and Karen Clark-Sheard, infamous voice in the world (no matter what genre of music). Kierra is a master builder. She is a singer, songwriter, actress, activist, entrepreneur, and business owner. She was a judge on BET's Sunday Best, founder of BRL (Bold! Right! Life!) - a movement for young adults, and she has her Bachelor's degree in English. Kierra saw the opportunities presented, was ready for them, and seized them. I submit that discipline is transferrable. Being a professional singer requires hard work, dedication, consistency, taking criticism, confidence, and the desire to learn... the list goes on. Those same skills that she honed as a singer transferred to other ventures. (Note: don't get too caught up on where you start, it is all about the finish line). Kierra laid the foundation, and started to build. I believe she is a great steward over what she has, which allows her to be entrusted with more. There is a verse for that (SMILE.) This next verse is going to be a long read, but it makes the point so I had to put the entire parable here. Take a deep breath and read (LOL):

> "Again, it will be like a man going on a journey, who called his servants and entrusted his wealth to them. To one he gave five bags of gold, to another two bags, and to another one bag, each according to his ability. Then he went on his journey. The man who had received five bags of gold went at once and put his money to work and gained five bags more. So also, the one with two bags of gold gained two more. But the man who had received one bag went off, dug a hole in the ground and hid his master's money. "After a long time the master of those servants returned and settled accounts with them. The man who had received five bags of gold brought the other five. 'Master,' he said, 'you entrusted me with five bags of gold. See, I have gained five more.' "His master replied, 'Well done, good and faithful servant! You have been faithful with a few things; I will put you in charge of many things. Come and share your master's happiness!' "The man with two bags of gold also came. 'Master,' he said, 'you entrusted me with two bags of gold; see, I have gained two more.' "His master replied, 'Well done, good and faithful servant! You have been faithful with a few things; I will put you in charge of many things. Come and share your master's happiness!' "Then the man who had received one bag of gold came. 'Master,' he said, 'I knew that you are a hard man, harvesting where you

> have not sown and gathering where you have not scattered seed. So I was afraid and went out and hid your gold in the ground. See, here is what belongs to you.' "His master replied, 'You wicked, lazy servant! So you knew that I harvest where I have not sown and gather where I have not scattered seed? Well then, you should have put my money on deposit with the bankers, so that when I returned I would have received it back with interest. "'So take the bag of gold from him and give it to the one who has ten bags. For whoever has will be given more, and they will have an abundance. Whoever does not have, even what they have will be taken from them. And throw that worthless servant outside, into the darkness, where there will be weeping and gnashing of teeth." (Matthew 25:14-30 NIV).

That parable is rich with principles, but I want you to grasp a few nuggets out of it. First, take what you have, and do something productive with it. Second, don't bury your gifts expecting something miraculous to happen to it. Next, when you take responsibility and are accountable for what you have it, opens the door for more to come your way. Lastly, be faithful with what is given to you. Always keep in mind and ask yourself, "How can I build upon this?" - Whatever "this" is, to you. I wholeheartedly desire that you live and maximize an abundant life.

Maximize

Challenge:

We are at the end of our relay race, and have finished with "Live and Maximize an Abundant Life". Recall that Jesus came that we might have life and have it abundantly (John 10:10b). So my challenge for you is to change your mind, actually, renew it. Romans 12:2 (NIV) says, "Do not conform to the pattern of this world, but be transformed by the renewing of your mind. Then you will be able to test and approve what God's will is—his good, pleasing and perfect will." Live with an abundant mentality today. Remove all negative talk and negative people from your life. Have the courage to say no to those things and people who do not mimic the Word of God. Be content. Don't look at others from the perspective of what you don't have. Take joy in 'you'! When you get up EVERY morning put on your faith glasses. Commune with the Father – that will help start your day off right. Girl, get off your technology and hone your craft. Don't waste your time on activities that will not produce fruit in your life. Practice, take a class, get a life coach, get a mentor, and utilize discipline. Do all those things and more so that you can be prepared when opportunities come your way. Lastly, build upon what you have. Never minimize your present location and situation. God can and will use everything in your life. Don't get too focused on certain things, and instead just stay focused on the right things. Keep building, and just make sure that you are building on the right and firm foundation.

Ebony's Corner:

As a young Christian woman I believed that I was to lead a low key, not too bold, and in some instances, pauper-like life. It just seemed like I was taught (or I absorbed the displayed demonstrations) that Christians were to have a certain attitude towards material possessions, money, and success. So, honestly, I was almost ashamed and often felt guilty to have a desire for anything that was above meek. That changed when I started to get into a Word church that taught the Bible from a victorious standpoint, and I started to shift my mindset. I am not saying that God wants every person to have a Bentley, but He does want us to have an abundant life (John 10:10b). So my question became, "What is my abundant life?" I got past material possessions, (those are nice though) and wanted to embrace other attributes. Seriously, I had stinking thinking about myself. Believing that I was special or could mean something to someone on a relevant level was weird to me. It was like – who am I? However, the more I embraced that God loved me and He created me for a purpose, the more I started to move out of the low state. Full disclosure: There are times I get in that lowly place, but I have the tools to get out of it. I know my gifts, talents, and abilities and I begin to go in "my closet" and perfect them. (Note: You cannot tell everyone everything about what God is preparing you for. Some people cannot handle the vision, because the vision was not given to them. Be wise with sharing your moves with people -- and that may include some of your family members too.) In my preparation season, I read a lot and watched a lot of relevant videos. I went back to school and got a Master of Arts in

Organizational Leadership. I am still building, but I have disciplined myself enough to be prepared so that when opportunities come I am ready to seize them.

Conclusion

My prayer is that this short read has been valuable, thoughtful, engaging, and life changing. My hope is that you will take what was written in this book, and put legs to them. Let me provide the reason you need to take action today – GOD LOVES YOU! Even when you feel like no one loves you, not even yourself, GOD LOVES YOU DEEPLY. Ephesians 1:3-4 (AMP) says, "Blessed and worthy of praise be the God and Father of our Lord Jesus Christ, who has blessed us with every spiritual blessing in the heavenly realms in Christ, just as [in His love] He chose us in Christ [actually selected us for Himself as His own] before the foundation of the world, so that we would be holy [that is, consecrated, set apart for Him, purpose-driven] and blameless in His sight." That is great news! He chose you, my sister, before the foundations of the world. Shout about that! God then, in His immense love for you, did John 3:16: "For God so [greatly] loved and dearly prized the world, that He [even] gave His [One and] only begotten Son, so that whoever believes and trusts in Him [as Savior] shall not perish, but have eternal life (AMP)." If you have never believed before, let today be that day that you begin. God is waiting on you with open arms to love on you in a way that surpasses understanding. He loves you when you are up and when you are down. He loves the REAL YOU. Please accept His love and walk into an eternal salvation. If you have already accepted Jesus Christ as your

Savior, but are not living and obeying His Word - please make your turn and get back on the path. God has extended grace. He has forgiven you and welcomes you back. Don't you remember the story of the prodigal son? Let me remind you: Luke 15:20-24 (NIV), "So he got up and went to his father. "But while he was still a long way off, his father saw him and was filled with compassion for him; he ran to his son, threw his arms around him and kissed him. "The son said to him, 'Father, I have sinned against heaven and against you. I am no longer worthy to be called your son.' "But the father said to his servants, 'Quick! Bring the best robe and put it on him. Put a ring on his finger and sandals on his feet. Bring the fattened calf and kill it. Let's have a feast and celebrate. For this son of mine was dead and is alive again; he was lost and is found.' So they began to celebrate." Repent my dear sister, and put on your robe!

I am not saying that following this book will instantly make your life marvelous like a movie, but I am saying that following these principles will allow for it. Desire to live a life that is liking to God. You can be awesome, gorgeous, intelligent, and courageous all while being a Woman of God. Don't be ashamed of who God has called you to be. Fall in love with your Daddy. Talk with Him, commune with Him, and worship Him. Don't neglect that personal relationship with Him. Girl, discover who you really are! You were not created to be a carbon copy, be the original. So why not be the best you? Discover why you were put on this Earth, and operate in it. DO IT, my sister. To do your gifting, you must allow the Holy Spirit to flow in and out of you. The Holy Spirit is there to guide, not to spook you. As you are grooving in your lane of purpose, you can live and maximize an abundant life. Two of the biggest tips I can give are to prepare for your season -- because baby it is coming -- and be a master builder. Stay in building mode.

Don't allow these nuggets to just be for you! Please get another book for your friend or family member. After all, sharing is caring, so share the wealth. I love you with the love of Christ, and I cannot wait to hear what God is doing in your lives. Blessings!

14 Day Devotional

I want to thank you so much for taking the time to read, re-read, take notes, and take more notes. It is my prayer that you have proactively utilized this book as a tool to help guide you on your personal relationship journey with Jesus Christ, so that you can lead a Godly successful life. If throughout this book you have said "Yes" to Him, then I am so excited for you. If this is your first "YES," then let me be the first to say, "Welcome to the family of God. If this is your second "YES," then let me be the first to say to you, "Welcome back to the family." No matter where you are in your journey, I want to give you another resource to help you stay engaged and excited throughout your passage. The forthcoming pages include a 14-day devotional. These devotionals provide a specific spiritual reading for fourteen days. The topics are broad in scope; however, they are relevant in nature. Life has a funny way of giving you what you need at each very moment, and constantly makes deposits in your life to be used for a later date. As you apply what you read in the earlier chapters, let these devotionals be the catalyst to get you started with eagerness to build upon your personal relationship with your Lord and Savior. Read the scripture and devotional, and truly apply the application thought. God is waiting on you, so let's begin your journey.

– Ebony

Day 1

The Call to Courage: Don't be Afraid of God's Assignment for Your Life

> *"Have I not commanded you? Be strong and of good courage; do not be afraid, nor be dismayed, for the Lord your God is with you wherever you go."*
>
> ***Joshua 1:9 NKJV***

Nothing happens in our lives apart from being courageous. In the text, Joshua is carrying on after the passing of Moses. God begins to give Joshua a pep talk. In this pep talk, He tells Joshua to be brave, courageous, and daring. God tells Joshua to be strong and of good courage, and He gives Joshua the best reason why he can. Because of God's presence, Joshua does not have to be afraid or dismayed. I hope this is speaking to you. Maybe you have been given a hefty assignment, and you are not sure how you are going to do it. Put yourself in the shoes of Joshua and receive this verse. God is with you my dear sister.

Application Thought:

What has God called you to do and you have not done it because of discouragement or lack of boldness?

Day 2

It's Working - Everything is Working for the Good

And we know that all things work together for good to those who love God, to those who are the called according to His purpose.
Romans 8:28 NKJV

Romans 8:28 is a popular scripture that a lot of Christians use in times of peril. Many times, we do not understand how a troubled marriage, a bad financial situation, or an unwise decision could work for our good. You may have questioned every hurt, pain, disappointment, or sadness, but it is working. To what end does all things work? For your good to those who love God, to those who are the called according to His purpose. Do you love God? Are you called according to His purpose? I love pineapple upside down cake. The ingredients for this cake include:

- Butter or margarine
- Brown sugar
- Sliced pineapples in juice
- Maraschino cherries
- All-purpose flour
- Granulated sugar
- Shortening
- Baking powder
- Salt
- Milk
- Egg

Now separately these ingredients may not be good, sound good, look good, or taste good. But when these ingredients are mixed up, and put in a hot oven for a certain period of time, the results are GOOD. The same with you. You may not understand everything that has happened in your past. Why the molestation, why the bankruptcy, why the strained relationships, why the dissolution of the marriage, why getting passed over for jobs? But, my dear sister it is working. Stay in the oven a little longer.

Application Thought:

Be assured that every detail in your life is working into something good.

Day 3

Redemption - God Redeems

Let the redeemed of the Lord say so
Whom He has redeemed from the hand of the enemy.
Psalms 107:2 NKJV

One definition of redeem is to buy back or to make something that is bad, better, or more acceptable. Have you done some things in your life that you wish you had the power to redeem yourself from? You wanted to bury your head in the sand because it wasn't looking too good? Or, maybe you got yourself caught up with someone or some things that you wanted to be brought back from? The great news is that God has redemptive power and has the ability to redeem us from ourselves and from the hands of the enemy. Christopher Gardner's story was told on the big screen by Will Smith in the critically acclaimed movie, *The Pursuit of Happyness.* Chris was a salesman who fell on challenging times, and became homeless with his young son. He had a chance encounter that landed him an unpaid internship along with others who were competing for the only paid position. Chris and his son experienced many obstacles, but Chris stayed focus, was determined, and gave his best efforts at all times. In the end, he earned the position and became very successful. Even when things didn't seem like it would be great Chris kept working and pushing. Even when his back was against the wall, sleeping in shelters, not knowing where his next meal could come from he kept going. I'm sure there were people in his life that turned their backs on home, talked about him, threw him under the bus, but he never missed a beat. Chris recalled that it wasn't by his might but by God's. God has redemptive power.

Application Thought:

Never give up because God redeems.

Day 4

Priorities - Kingdom Living

But seek first the kingdom of God and His righteousness, and all these things shall be added to you.
Matthew 6:33 NKJV

In **Matthew 6:33** Jesus tells us to seek first the Kingdom of Heaven and all things shall be given unto you. In our daily lives, it is so easy to lose focus on our service to the Lord and to get wrapped up in the material things and the cares of this world. His Kingdom should be priority. Well what is His Kingdom? It is His way of doing things - simply stated. There is a command to pursue and seek the Kingdom. More than having an awareness of that God is first and greater than other sources, we are commanded to seek His kingdom. We are commanded to do things the way He would do things. There was a popular bracelet that people used to wear. On it were the initials W.W.J.D. This reminded a person to ask themselves the question - What Would Jesus Do? - before they would act or react in situations. Our seeking is volitional and intentional. God does not force us to seek Him. The Bible says His spirit draws us (John 6:44), but He does not force us. We do not seek God by accident. Seeking is a deliberate choice to search for God with the eyes of your heart. Seek God's way of doing things and not get caught up on fleshly, surface things.

Application Thought:

Be clear on your priorities, if it's not Christ, rearrange them.

Day 5

The Early Days - Small Beginnings

"Who dares despise the day of small things, since the seven eyes of the Lord that range throughout the earth will rejoice when they see the chosen capstone in the hand of Zerubbabel?"
Zechariah 4:10 NIV

The purpose of the book of Zechariah is to encourage the people who had recently returned from exile. Their faith in God was weak, and they were not motivated to build the temple. They were in the rebuilding stage and he implored them to not despise the days of small beginnings. You may be in that place of despising your situation. Maybe you despise your upbringing. Quite possibly you despise the little you had or even to get by. You are tired of robbing Peter to pay Paul. Author, J.K. Rowling is a testament of small beginnings. She had a somewhat decent childhood, but after her divorce her life took a turn downward. She found herself jobless and in a state of depression. She began to write and eventually the first of the Harry Potter books was birthed. She is now the ninth-best-selling fiction author of all time - selling over 500 million books. Don't despise the small beginnings because the power of God can render the smallest of instruments productive of His greatest work.

Application Thought:

What in your life has been deemed as "small" that has been despised in your life? Change your attitude and rejoice in the works of God.

Day 6

Clean Heart - Create, Renew, and Restore

> *Create in me a clean heart, O God,*
> *And renew a steadfast spirit within me.*
> *Do not cast me away from Your presence*
> *And do not take Your Holy Spirit from me.*
> *Restore to me the joy of Your salvation*
> *And sustain me with a willing spirit.*
> ***Psalm 51:10-12***

David wrote this Psalm when Nathan the prophet came to him after he had sinned with Bathsheba. David realized that he had sinned and most importantly sinned against God. This psalm was written out of guilt and repentance with the desire to be forgiven. Have you done some things in your life that you knew or realized were wrong? That it was a sin against man and God? The question then becomes how do you move on? How do you get to a place of forgiveness, and having a slate that is wiped clean? That process can be done in three steps. First you want to create a new heart. This is done by having a clear understanding that the current heart is rotten, and you need a new heart that is pure and righteous. Secondly you want to renew your spirit. Life can beat you down, and it is sometimes not that obvious that your spirit needs a charge, a jolt. Lastly, you must restore the joy. Salvation is the security we have in Christ. It is the true foundation. As much as you admire a new car, we know that when it is dirty it is not that appealing. Once it is washed and detailed then a person may view it with a deeper appreciation. There are times when you have to clean your heart.

Application Thought:

Desire a pure, clean heart so that you can be effective for the Kingdom of God.

Day 7

It's Not Over - God Will Finish What He Has Started

Being confident of this very thing, that He who has begun a good work in you will complete it until the day of Jesus Christ.
Philippians 1:6 NKJV

Our lives are often filled with loose ends. We have home improvement tasks that we've begun but not finished, books cracked open, but not completed, promises made but not kept, intentions begun but not followed through on. Our lives are often replete with would've, should've, and could've. But the good news is that God always finishes what he starts. Paul begins the verse by saying he is confident. Confidence is vital. We can have confidence in others and ourselves but along the journey there will be some failures. Thank God, He is trustworthy, faithful, and never fails. The God-work that has been started will get completed. The vision that God impregnated you with will birth. God is true to His word. It has to complete because **Isaiah 55:11** says, *So shall My word be that goes forth from My mouth; It shall not return to Me void, But it shall accomplish what I please, And it shall prosper in the thing for which I sent it.* Put your head down, dig your heels in, and keep going.

Application Thought:

Be confident that God will complete what He has started in your life.

Day 8

Putting in Work - Attitude About Our Work

And whatever you do, do it heartily, as to the Lord and not to men.
Colossians 3:23

We're always working at something or on something. Since that is a part of our lives, it makes perfect sense that the Word of God provides clarity around it. Colossians 3:23 breaks it down by saying Whatever you do - so whatever the task, whatever the work, or whatever the relationship. It speaks to whatever that we do. The scripture says - Work heartily. No matter the work we do we are supposed to do it heartily. The International Standard Bible Encyclopedia defines heartily as "out of the soul". So, in essence, you must work with everything that you have. There should not be any slack or laziness, but active zeal. As for the Lord, work heartily, as if you are working for Him, and not for men. No matter the situation, we can find satisfaction with our work when God is the priority and focus. When we work for Christ there is an eternal reward. Realizing that we are serving the Lord Christ (v.24) should change our perspective of our work. When we're working (whether at a job or relationship), we have the opportunity to serve others, which could show them the character of Jesus. There must be an epiphany that reminds us that it is not about self, but it is about Christ and how He is working through others to serve others.

Application Thought:

Change your attitude about your work. Do it for Christ.

Day 9

Overcomer - Despite the Trouble, Jesus Overcame the World

> *"I have told you these things, so that in me you may have peace. In this world you will have trouble. But take heart! I have overcome the world."*
>
> ***John 16:33 NIV***

No one has to think very hard to come up with a list of troubles, right? Trouble is all around us. Jesus said that it would be. He said, "In this world you will have trouble." There are stories of troubles written in the newspapers, magazines, on the internet, and told on the television. There are stories of troubles in all our lives. What kind of troubles are in your city, state, and country? What kind of troubles are in your life? Write down a few. The list that you just compiled probably looks overwhelming. Let's hear what God has to say. Jesus says that there will be trouble, but He also says, "be of good cheer!" This means to be confident or bold in an inconvenient situation. Be brave! You've got this! Be fearless! You can do this! The great news is that we don't have to be brave alone. We aren't fighting troubles alone. We can be courageous because Jesus showed us how to be. He chose to die on that cross for our sins and rose in three days to show that He can overcome ANYTHING!!!! Jesus did it and we can too, with His help.

Application Thought:

Stop focusing on the trouble and focus on the One who can help you overcome.

Day 10

Don't Give Up - The Right Stuff

And let us not grow weary while doing good, for in due season we shall reap if we do not lose heart.
Galatians 6:9 NKJV

It can be tough doing what is "good," especially when you do not see any results. It can become a little depressing when you are living for Christ, and there is nothing to show for it. But we must have confidence in knowing that we will reap what we've sewn. A farmer knows that whatever he plants will reap when it's harvest time. They are very diligent in taking care of the plant - with water, sunlight, fertilizer, and the right environment. Regardless if the plant doesn't seem like it's growing, the farmer knows that in due season it will reap. Much like the farmer, we must be patient knowing that we will reap the harvest if we do not give up. I know you may be tired, ready to throw in the towel, but be confident in knowing that your prayer, meditation, and obedience to the Word will reap a harvest in God's timing.

Application Thought:

If you are in the right environment, doing the right things, your harvest is coming.

Day 11

Privileges of Being Righteous - You Have Rights

But in that coming day
no weapon turned against you will succeed.
You will silence every voice
raised up to accuse you.
These benefits are enjoyed by the servants of the Lord;
their vindication will come from me.
I, the Lord, have spoken!
Isaiah 54:17 NLT

A weapon is designed to inflict pain against someone. There are weapons - people, places, and things - that are designed specifically for you to inflict pain, to divert your purpose, or to make you think less of yourself. Think about those weapons that have tried to attack you. Could it be a job situation, money issues, or relationships drama? There may be more to list. The weapons will come, but they will not succeed. If you were fighting your own battles the weapons quite possibly would defeat you. But, because you serve a powerful God who is strong and mighty (Psalm 24:8) the fight is unfair. Have you watched an unmatched fight before? Don't you feel bad for the smaller, weaker person? The same is true for your situation. Because you are righteous, the weapons that are coming your way will not take you out. You have rights that set you up for success.

Application Thought:

As you face the weapons and engage in the battles of life, set your heart and hope on the final outcome. It's going to end well for you.

Day 12

Combatting Stress - Winning Anxiety

When anxiety was great within me,
your consolation brought me joy
Psalm 94:19 NKJV

Life brings so much pressure which can invoke anxiety and worry. In our minds, we have so much to worry about – family, job security, financial surety, health concerns – that causes our minds to race at a mile a minute. Our bodies experience the flight or fight response which makes some prone to anxiety. This verse should convey calmness, because God's comfort brings joy. Joy is so sweet because it surpasses the feeling of happiness. John Piper defines Christian joy as a good feeling in the soul, produced by the Holy Spirit, as he causes us to see the beauty of Christ in the word and in the world. God offers relief from anxiety and worry by giving us joy. The latter portion of **Nehemiah 8:10** says, *The joy of the Lord is your strength.* By allowing God to comfort you with his joy, it will cause you to be strong and look at those situations in your life, and tackle them with a different attitude because you have the Lord with you.

Application Thought:

The Lord wants you to live in freedom and joy. May God help you to relinquish your worries so you can experience His consolation.

Day 13

Wisdom - Ask for It

But if any of you lacks wisdom, let him ask of God, who gives to all generously and without reproach, and it will be given to him. 6 But he must ask in faith without any doubting, for the one who doubts is like the surf of the sea, driven and tossed by the wind.
James 1:5-6 NASB

With so many decisions to be made at home, at work, and extracurricular activities do you ever consider asking God to guide your thoughts? Do you ever think to ask for direction in EVERYTHING that you do? Many situations require God's wisdom, yet we do not ask or we ask with some doubt in our hearts. You must ask in faith and not doubt that God will hear and answer. Well what is wisdom, and why should you ask for it? Wisdom is the correct application of knowledge. So, it is knowing something, but doing the right thing with what you know. You can know that oven mits are supposed to be used when using an oven. But if you don't put on the oven mitts while the oven is in use, the knowledge of the mitts is useless. Many times we are faced with challenges that, without correctly applying the knowledge, can produce a disastrous situation. His word says that when we ask Him, He will give liberally to us. He doesn't hold it back. He longs for us to have His wisdom. We should pray daily for God to give us His wisdom, so that when we are faced with demanding situations throughout the day, we will know how to handle it.

Application Thought:

God's wisdom is needed every day so daily pray for it to be given liberally.

Day 14

A Time for Everything - Stop Watching Your Clock

To everything there is a season,
A time for every purpose under heaven
Ecclesiastes 3:1 NKJV

Have you ever noticed how much we complain about time? In certain situations, we desire more time whereas other situations the time can't go fast enough. This verse reminds us that every season of life is purposeful. You will face season of great difficulty, and times of great jubilee. You'll experience both seasons of demanding work, and seasons of reaping the harvest. In every season, God wants to teach something new about who He is, and how great His love is toward us. Your attitude toward life changes when you learn to appreciate every season, good times and tough times, as opportunities to grow closer to God. As you learn to trust Him, you will find yourself a lot less worried about what's coming next. Each season - spring, summer, fall, and winter - has its purpose. As much as a person may not like winter, without it the ecosystem would be thrown off. Rest in God's capacity that your seasons have purpose.

Application Thought:

Look for God in every season of your life. He has a message for you.

References:

[a] Lifeway Christian Resources (2003) "Spiritual Gifts Survey." http://www.lifeway.com/lwc/files/lwcF_MYCS_030526_Spiritual_Gifts_Survey.pdf

[b] "Matthew Henry" Conservapedia: The Trusting Encyclopedia. 27 July 2016. http://www.conservapedia.com/Matthew_Henry#Ministry

[c] Rees, Erik. S.H.A.P.E.: Finding and Fulfilling Your Unique Purpose for Life. Zondervan, 2008.

[d] Lee, Jimison. (2010) "Exploiting your 4×100 meter Relay Personnel." http://speedendurance.com/2010/11/28/exploiting-your-4x100-meter-relay-personnel/

[e] "Life Expectancy" Centers For Disease Control and Prevention. 3 May 2017. https://www.cdc.gov/nchs/fastats/life-expectancy.htm

About the Author

Ebony Robinson, MOL, is a minister, speaker, certified life coach, mentor, and author. She currently resides in Ypsilanti, MI, but was born and raised in Fort Wayne, IN. Robinson owns and operates 320, LLC. – A company with a mission to challenge the structural thinking of people and organizations, and to change the narrative of how change is seen. She serves alongside her husband, Pastor Jason Robinson, at Reach Church in Ypsilanti, where she is the Chief Ministry Officer. With a strong calling on her life to minister to all people, she is specifically drawn to women. She is a proud mother to four beautiful children.

Ministering to Women. Cultivating Purpose. Unleashing Power.

91507462R00069

Made in the USA
Columbia, SC
21 March 2018